RAILROAD TYCOON II ™

Official Strategy Guide

Gathering of Developers
2700 Fairmount Street
Dallas, TX 75201

www.godgames.com

Railroad Tycoon II–Official Strategy Guide

Published by: Gathering of Developers
2700 Fairmount Street
Dallas, TX 75201

ISBN: 1-892817-00-4
Printed in the United States of America
99 00 01   10 9 8 7 6 5 4 3 2 1

Contents at a Glance

Contents

Introduction

Railroad Tycoon II is the sequel to the highly successful game, *Railroad Tycoon*. Like its predecessor, it gives players the opportunity to roll the dice as a railroad mogul in the development of their own railroad—something only a handful of men were able to do historically.

Although the general premise is the same, *Railroad Tycoon II* includes added features, AI changes, interface restructuring, and both campaign modes and stand-alone scenarios that will challenge even the most seasoned robber baron. In short, *Railroad Tycoon II* is a different game, with improvements and changes in virtually every area.

HOW TO USE THIS BOOK

This strategy guide is designed to help you get the most out of playing *Railroad Tycoon II*. It's full of useful tips, tactics, and information—all designed to give you the inside scoop:

> **Part I**, *Railroad Tycoon II* Basics, includes general information about the game, the underlying economic model that makes everything tick, and some quick tips and strategies for various areas of the game.
>
> **Part II**, Men, Machines, and Industries, lists reference information on the tycoons and managers in the game, as well as facts on the trains. This section also contains detailed information on "best practices" for building your railroad.
>
> **Part III**, The Lay of the Land, covers Bronze, Silver, and Gold medal strategies for every campaign in the game, as well as the stand-alone maps.
>
> **Part IV**, Running with the Big Dogs, contains tips for multiplayer *Railroad Tycoon II*, as well as quick tips for the multiplayer maps in the game.
>
> **Part V**, Creating Your Own Playgrounds, provides an overview of the map editor, as well as details on the event editor that enable you to set up complex events for your maps.
>
> **Part VI**, The Real Tycoons, includes an interview with Phil Steinmeyer, designer of *Railroad Tycoon II*, as well as profiles of the PopTop Software team members.
>
> Finally, the appendixes provide a good source of reference information that you can access at-a-glance, including cheat codes.

So fire up your computer, get into the game, and use this guide to help you get the most from this soon-to-be-classic game. All aboard—it's time to get this train out of the station.

PART I

RAILROAD TYCOON II BASICS

RAILROAD TYCOON II GIVES YOU THE OPPORTUNITY TO BUILD, MANAGE, AND PROFIT FROM A SPRAWLING RAILROAD EMPIRE-- SOMETHING MOST OF US DON'T GET TO DO EVERY DAY. THIS PART PROVIDES A SOLID INTRODUCTION TO THE GAME AND ITS INNER WORKINGS.

1

The World of Railroad Tycoon II

THIS CHAPTER IS DESIGNED TO GIVE YOU

A GOOD WORKING KNOWLEDGE OF THE BASIC

FACTORS INVOLVED IN PLAYING RAILROAD

TYCOON II. AFTER READING THIS CHAPTER,

YOU WILL HAVE GAINED A SOLID WORKING

KNOWLEDGE OF ALL THE BASIC FACTORS

INVOLVED IN BUILDING YOUR RAILROAD

EMPIRE.

BREAKING IT DOWN

The world of *Railroad Tycoon II* revolves around three segments that are all intimately tied together: infrastructure, management, and finance. *Infrastructure* has to do with all construction details, such as starting a company, laying and upgrading track, building and upgrading stations, and buying trains. This is the beginning point for everything else in the game.

Once you have your infrastructure in place, you have to manage it, using the tools in the game. *Management* includes setting up train consists (cargo loads), managing traffic, buying industries, monitoring goodwill in other territories, and making the decisions about where and how to expand.

Management doesn't occur in a vacuum. The primary challenge of *Railroad Tycoon II* is that you must build an infrastructure and manage it within a financial framework. There are real consequences for mismanagement in the real world, and these are accurately reflected in the game. *Finance* includes company finances (incurring debt, issuing stock, and maximizing shareholder revenues) as well as personal finances (managing your personal stock portfolio, net worth maximization).

In reality, the distinction between these game segments is rather blurry, since you are tasked with *managing* the *infrastructure* of your empire within a *financial* framework. In the following sections, we'll explore how these segments are all tied together.

INFRASTRUCTURE

Think of the infrastructure as the building block of the game. You need to build tracks and stations and buy upgrades and buildings before you can start with the day-to-day operation of your railroad. Most of these transactions can be done with the game paused.

> IN GENERAL, IT'S WISE TO PAUSE YOUR GAME FOR TRANSACTIONS. OTHERWISE, YOU WILL BE WASTING VALUABLE TIME, SINCE THE GAME CLOCK IS TICKING AWAY, AS YOU'RE TRYING TO DECIDE WHERE TO START BUILDING AND WHAT TO UPGRADE. PAUSE THE GAME AS SOON AS THE BRIEFING APPEARS TO AVOID WASTED TIME, THEN RESUME PLAY ONCE YOU HAVE YOUR FIRST TRAINS READY TO ROLL.

STARTING A COMPANY

Your first step is to start a company. Unless you plan to strictly play the stock market, you must start a company in order to play the scenarios. Starting a company is very straightforward—simply double-click on the Start a New Company tab in the Central List Box. The Start New Company dialog box will appear.

When you start a company, you must choose how much money you will personally put into the company, and how much you will accept from outside investors. The more money you put in, the more outside investors will be willing to put in. Usually, you can push both sliders all the way to the right to maximize your starting capital, but some scenarios will limit your options.

You can also select a name and logo for your company—these are both purely cosmetic, and you can change them at any time from the Company Detail Screen.

LAYING YOUR FIRST TRACK

Once you've started a company, it's time to get down to business. The first thing you need to do is lay some track. Select two cities or towns—preferably two that have a good concentration of passengers or other cargo—then connect them with track by clicking on the Lay Track button (it's the button that looks like railroad tracks) in the Main Window.

Once you've clicked on the Lay Track button, click at one of your destinations, then hold the mouse button down and drag the track to the other destination. Once there, release the mouse button and the track will be laid.

The numbers that float above the track as you lay it serve two important functions. There are two types of numbers—Cost numbers (white), and Grade numbers (green, yellow, or red). Cost numbers are white and appear above the proposed track. The cost will vary based upon the terrain you are trying to lay track over, and the grade of the proposed track. The total cost of the entire length of track will appear below the Central List Box.

Grade numbers come in three shades—green, yellow, and red—and each color appears based upon the grade of the stretch of track:

- **Green numbers** appear when the proposed track's grade is optimal. Try to keep all your track in the green as you lay it—trains will move much faster along track that has a low grade.
- **Yellow numbers** indicate track with marginal grades. Do your best to avoid these areas by taking track around them if at all possible.
- **Red numbers** indicate prohibitive grades. These are grades that will stop a train in its tracks—literally. Avoid these grades at all costs—they will kill even the most lucrative routes.

> YOU CAN STOP LAYING TRACK BY CLICKING ON THE LAY TRACK BUTTON AGAIN. HOWEVER, DON'T LET GO OF THE MOUSE BUTTON UNTIL YOU ARE OVER THE LAY TRACK BUTTON, OR YOU'LL LAY TRACK YOU'D RATHER NOT PUT DOWN.

BUILDING STATIONS

In order to pick up cargo, trains must stop at stations. Now that you have some track laid, you need to put stations at each end of your track.

Select the Build a New Station button, and the Center List Box will change to display three station choices—Small, Medium, and Large. You will also see several choices for the architecture of your stations.

Each station type collects resources from the area surrounding them, just as if those areas are bringing resources to the station for shipment. This collection zone varies by station size—small stations collect from a relatively small area, medium stations collect from a somewhat larger one, and large stations collect from the largest surrounding area.

When you're placing stations, there are a few guidelines to follow:

- **Choose the right size for the area**—It's a waste of money to put down a large or medium station when a small one will do. Place your track as close to the resource as you can so you can be conservative with station size.

- **Span multiple areas with large stations**—A large station can be placed between two resources or cities so that it overlaps both of them. This is also an excellent way to reach areas that would be more costly otherwise (due to bridges, terrain, and so on).

- **Multiple stations can collect from the same area**—If a parallel set of track is laid, you can put a station very close to another one. In effect, the stations will split the total cargo available, and it will be available on a first-come, first-served basis.

Once you have your stations in place, you can enter the Station Detail Screen and upgrade them with various improvements. For more information, see Chapter 5: Building Your Railroad Empire.

BUYING TRAINS

With two stations in place, you're ready to buy a train to haul cargo between them. Click on the Purchase a New Train button (it's the button that looks like a train—pretty obvious, but hey, we had to tell you).

The purchase dialog will appear with a list of all currently available locomotives. Select one, and its details will appear on the right side of the screen. If it appears to be the one you wish to purchase, click Purchase to buy it.

When buying trains, be careful which ones you purchase:

- **Tailor each train to its route**—If the grade the train will be travelling is steep, be sure to choose a good performer on steep grades. If the grade is flat, then select one that does well in that situation.

- **Buy trains with average or better reliability**—Breakdowns will occur more frequently for trains with below average numbers in reliability. Buy them at your own risk.

- **Expensive doesn't equal best**—Don't plunk down cash for the most expensive train in all cases; it may not be the best buy for your route or situation. You'll repeat these steps over and over, but not without some of the ones that follow in the next section.

MANAGEMENT

Management involves taking the infrastructure you've built, and using it to turn a profit for your company. This is the most complex portion of the game, since it crosses so many other areas. To keep things simple, you should distinguish between:

- **Train/Consists management**—Selecting cargo for each train, optimized for the highest profits per run
- **Expansion management**—Growing your railroad properly and planning for future growth
- **Company management**—Taking the necessary steps to build your company, increase return on investment for shareholders, and generally run a profitable, growing business

TRAIN/CONSISTS MANAGEMENT

Once you've purchased a train, it's time to assign its consist, or cargo cars. *Railroad Tycoon II* enables you to do this every time a train is in a station, and in the early going, you'll need to be sure you do this every time.

After the purchase dialog disappears, you'll be taken to the consists management screen. This screen has the map of the scenario on the right side. From this map, select the two end-points of your run. They will appear on the left half of the screen. Double-click on each one in turn, and the right side of the screen will become the Cars List.

You can add any car to the train's consist for this station, but unless you select from the Cars Supplied by this Station grouping, you won't be hauling any cargo. At the bottom of the screen, you can see what cargo is available (Supply) and what that particular station demands.

> THE NUMBER OF CARS SUPPLIED OR DEMANDED IS INDICATED BY THE NUMBER OF PICTURES OF THAT CAR ABOVE ITS PLACEHOLDER CAR.

Before picking cars for this consist, double-click the next station and check its Demands list. Now, return to the previous station and select from the available cars only those that are demanded by the second station. Repeat the process with the next station, and you should now have full consists for both stations.

Send the train on its way, and you'll turn a profit when it reaches the next station. There, it will load the consist you've indicated and return to its

starting point. This might seem simple, but if this were all there is to it, you'd get bored quickly. Following are a few tips for managing consists:

- **Keep trains below three cars initially**—In most cases, it's best to keep trains under three cars to keep their weight reasonable, and allow them to move quickly to their destinations. This is especially true with older trains (pre-1880).

- **Don't send a train out empty**—If your first station has no demand for the second station's cargo, find a third station that does and send the train there next. Too many empty runs will get you in trouble quickly.

- **Stations cannot store cargo from other stations**—You can't haul a cargo to one station, drop it off, and then haul it to the next station. You'll need to take the cargo to a station that demands it first.

EXPANSION MANAGEMENT

The next phase of railroad management is that of expanding your enterprise. Two stations and one train simply won't cut it—at least not if you expect to go down in history as one of the great tycoons, rather than "that guy who had a train."

Your first concern is where to expand. Look for:

- **Large cities**—In general, you can't go wrong if you place a station in a large city (New York, Buenos Aires, or Tokyo). Passenger and mail traffic will be high to and from the city, and it will demand almost all other cargo.

- **Look to cover a complete product cycle**—The home run in hauling cargo is to haul the initial component (Coal) to a secondary point (Steel Mill), then haul the finished product (Steel) to the next step (Tool and Die Factory), which is ideally located near the first step. One train can make your company a fortune with this kind of route.

- **Don't get ahead of yourself**—Maintaining track can get expensive. Don't lay track unless you are able to use it immediately. Long hauls of track will kill your expansion, unless you have enough short routes to offset the cost.

- **Stick to coastlines at first**—In most countries, cities are located along the coast, making it easy to haul cargo between them.

- **Snatch up short, lucrative routes**—It doesn't matter what the cargo is. If both ends demand the other's cargo, get them up and running quickly. Passenger routes of medium distance between cities work the same way.

Next, you need to look for other types of expansion. If you are playing on the Expert Industrial mode, you'll be able to buy industries around the map. When you're deciding to buy an industry:

- **Choose industries with Good or better profitability**—Don't buy industries that aren't doing well. The only exception is when you find one that you can easily make profitable yourself.

- **Buy industries on competitors' routes**—Nothing is sweeter than making money from your competitors' efforts. If you own a lucrative industry on one of their routes, they are making money for you with every load they haul.

- **Combine tactics to score big**—Combine the expansion tactic of hauling cargo to a complete industry cycle (Coal - Steel Mill - Steel - Tool and Die Factory) with buying industries. If you own all the industries you are hauling to and from along this vector, you'll really cash in.

The final type of management expansion is a merger with another company. While a large portion of a merger's tactics occur in the financial arena, deciding when to merge is strictly a measure of your analysis of a competitor's position.

The main criterion that decides whether you should attempt a merger is how much of the other company's stock you own. If you own none of it, don't try it unless you can pay top dollar. If, however, you own the majority of the company's shares, you are guaranteed to win, unless you vote against yourself—in which case you should seek professional help.

FINANCE

The financial portion of *Railroad Tycoon II* is the linchpin that the rest of the game hinges upon. If you do a phenomenal job of building your infrastructure and managing your railroad, you will still lose if you ignore the financial side of the game.

There are two sides to the financial picture and, depending upon the scenario, either or both of them will be important to your victory. The first is corporate finance, which is concerned with the financial picture of your company, and the second is personal finance, which basically tracks your ability to earn personal wealth.

CORPORATE FINANCES

The heart of managing corporate finances is the Company Detail Screen. To get there, double-click on your company from the Center List Box. There are several key areas to this corporate ledger:

- **Overview**—This tab provides at-a-glance information about your performance, your current manager, and a brief snapshot of your company's current status.

- **Income**—This is where you can view your income statement and compare revenues with expenses. In case you're a novice to financial management, the idea is for revenues to exceed expenses. If you open this page and see a lot of red (read negative) numbers, things aren't going well.

- **Balance**—Use the balance sheet to get a feel for your company's current equity position. The stronger your debt-to-equity ratio, the more likely your share price will rise along with your credit rating.

- **Territories**—This tab is where you can find out what your neighbors think about you. This is important, since you can't expand into territories you don't have rights in. It pays to be nice.
- **Finances**—This is the page you'll look up most often. Here, you can issue bonds and stock, buy back stock, manage company dividends, attempt mergers, and—if things get ugly—declare bankruptcy.

There's so much information in these screens, it can be a bit intimidating at first. Fortunately, you won't need to learn everything until late in the campaign scenarios. Actually, if you learn the Finances section, you will have picked up most of the skills you need.

Since the Finances tab of the ledger is so crucial, there are a few general tips that will help you as you start playing:

- **Issuing Bonds**—Never rely on bonds to finance your existing operations. Only incur debt when you can use it to expand to grab a lucrative route. Also, you usually don't need to worry about paying back your bonds— most of the campaigns end before 30 years, which is the payoff date on most bonds.
- **Issuing Stock**—Issuing stock drives your share price down. You should only do this when you plan on buying up the shares at the new, lower market price. Be sure to pause the game, then issue stock, and then buy it up. If you don't pause the game, the computer players will buy your stock before you can. Don't ever issue stock because you're desperate for cash.
- **Buy Back Stock**—Buying back stock from the market will drive your share price up. Unlike issuing stock, you can do this whenever you have the cash to afford to buy it. A high stock price will lead to greater personal wealth, and, if you're lucky, a stock split.
- **Change Dividend**—As chairman, you have some control over the dividend the company pays shareholders. As the company's largest shareholder, a higher dividend will increase your personal net worth. However, the board won't let you push the dividend too high, since it could leave the company unable to operate as effectively.
- **Attempt Merger**—When you feel that you have a good chance to take control of another company, either through surplus cash or smart investments, you can attempt a merger. The target company's shareholders will vote, and if they agree, then the merger is successful. Hint: If you are their majority shareholder, you will always win.
- **Declare Bankruptcy**—As in the real world, declaring bankruptcy is a devastating thing. You'll lose half your cash, your credit rating will go in the toilet, and you'll lose your slip at the yacht club. Still, if you need to cut your debt in half, and you have no other options, it's here for you. Don't do this unless you are truly desperate.

PERSONAL FINANCES

Last, but not least, personal finance rounds out our breakdown of the game's three major segments. There are only a few things you can do to affect personal finance, but if you do them well, the results will be easy to repeat.

If you take a look at the Player Detail Screen, which is accessed by double-clicking your character's name in the Central List Box, you'll see that not much information is contained here. You can view your cash on hand, stocks, and your purchasing power.

The next page lists your current stock holdings. You will rarely come to this page. In fact, most of your personal financial management will take place in the stock market. Click on the share of stock on the desk to enter the Stock Market Detail screen.

There are three actions you can perform in the stock market. For more discussion on these topics, see Chapter 5: Building Your own Railroad Empire.

> PURCHASING POWER IS CALCULATED BY ADDING YOUR CASH TO (OR SUBTRACTING YOUR LACK OF IT FROM) HALF YOUR STOCK VALUE.

- **Buying Stock**—If you have sufficient cash, this is a straightforward transaction. If not, then it's called buying on margin, which can be risky. Don't attempt it unless you know what you're doing.

- **Selling Stock**—Remember that all stock sales will drive share prices down, so don't unnecessarily sell your stocks unless you plan to buy more at the lower rate. Selling stock when you don't own it is called short selling, and is equally as risky as buying on margin.

- **View Corporate Info**—This allows you to see the corporation's position. Information on all companies in the game is available and includes largest shareholders as part of the mix. Make sure this is always you in your own company.

BRINGING IT ALL TOGETHER

Now that we've reviewed the basic three segments of the game—Infrastructure, Management, and Finance—it's time to pull it all together and make your mark on history. If you remember the structure we've laid out here, it will help you in your decisions throughout the game.

Remember that you can't rely on expertise in one area to give you victory. You have to become skilled in all three areas. The minute you abandon one is the minute that a competitor uses that one area to ambush you.

The computer's artificial intelligence (AI) can be brutal, but it will make mistakes. Don't underestimate its ability to work the stock market, especially on the Expert Financial Model. Make extensive use of the Pause key to avoid this problem.

The most important thing to remember is to take your time. Don't rush it—you'll probably spend many games scratching your head until everything clicks, but once it does, you'll be hooked.

The Economy

TO REALLY MAKE BIG PROFITS IN RAILROAD

TYCOON II, YOU'LL NEED TO UNDERSTAND

HOW THE ECONOMY WORKS, BOTH AT AN

OVERALL, MAP-WIDE LEVEL, AND IN THE SMALL

AREA WITHIN WHICH YOUR RAILROAD

OPERATES. MUCH OF YOUR OPERATIONAL AND

STOCK MARKET STRATEGY WILL NEED TO BE

TUNED TO FIT THE ECONOMY WITHIN WHICH

YOU'RE OPERATING. HERE'S A LOOK AT WHAT'S

GOING ON BEHIND THE SCENES IN THE

ECONOMY, AND HOW TO USE THIS KNOWLEDGE

TO ENRICH YOUR COMPANY AND YOURSELF.

THE OVERALL MAP ECONOMY

At the highest level, the prosperity of the map upon which you're playing is based on a number of global, map-wide parameters that are beyond your control. The biggest of these are the map setup, the starting year, and the current economic status.

FIGURE 2-1. A SAMPLE MAP

MAP SETUP

Obviously, all maps differ from each other in look and feel. Beyond the basic differences of varying coastlines, mountain ranges, and forests, each map has a unique economy, set up by the map's designer (Figure 2-1). In the map editor, there are a variety of tools that control which industries appear, where they appear, and how dense they are. These are used by the map designer to simulate the real economy of the area depicted. The exact distribution is determined randomly when the map is started, but if you restart the same map several times in a row, you'll definitely see trends.

For example, on the Eastern U.S. map, cotton appears in the Carolinas, auto factories appear in the upper Midwest (especially around Detroit), and so on. The impact of this is that certain maps lend themselves to certain strategies. For example, the map of China has a number of densely populated cities all located fairly close to each other in the broad central plain. These cities are easily connected, and the fastest way to get a jump in this scenario is to haul passengers and mail between these cities, adding industrial routes with the profits you earn. In South America, by contrast, big cities are fewer in number and more difficult to connect, but there is a broad area in Argentina densely packed with grain and cattle farms. Connect these farms and haul the cattle to a nearby meatpacking plant, and you'll make a fortune.

> IN GENERAL, FOR ANY NON-EUROPEAN SCENARIO STARTING AFTER 1900, FOCUS ON INDUSTRIES FIRST, AND ONLY RUN PASSENGERS OVER LINES ALREADY BUILT FOR YOUR INDUSTRIES. WATCH YOUR COSTS, AND REMOVE ANY TRAINS THAT AREN'T PROFITABLE.

STARTING YEAR

Shortly after the invention of the Iron Horse, railroads were the preferred method of transportation for passengers, and for virtually every type of cargo, as well. Railroads tended to be short, but with no other competition for overland routes, they became the dominant forms of transportation. However, new forms of transportation, notably the automobile and the airplane, carved away key cargoes from the railroads. Today, few passengers use railroads in North America, though they remain popular in Europe and other parts of the world. Most high value, priority cargoes—such as food and finished goods—rely on trucks for short hauls (less than 500 miles or so) and only travel via rail for longer hauls. Heavy commodities, such as coal and iron, still rely almost exclusively on rail transport.

In the game, you'll see a drop-off in passenger traffic in the 20th century, particularly in North America. You'll also see short hauls become less profitable, and you'll need to focus on long profitable runs, preferably with a different cargo available to haul back, so you can make money on both legs of the round trip.

> THERE IS NO UNIVERSAL BUILDING STRATEGY OR "BEST" CARGO—STUDY THE MAP AND BUILD ACCORDING TO THE INDUSTRIES PRESENT.

FIGURE 2-2. THE ECONOMY CONSTANTLY CHANGES.

ECONOMIC STATUS

The overall economy within each map swings cyclically up and down, just like the real-world economy (Figure 2-2). The player has no control over this—so many factors are involved that the performance of any one railroad (or even all of them) is negligible. The economy can be in any of these five states:

- Depression
- Recession
- Normal
- Prosperity
- Boom Times

It tends to change up or down a level every 6 to 18 months, often making a full swing from depression to boom times or back in about 5 years. The economy also has momentum, if it has just moved up a grade, it is probably more likely to move up another grade than to move back down.

The game's economic state affects these individual variables (which in turn can and should affect your strategy):

- **Cargo Generation Rate**—For every level up (or down) from normal, 8 percent more (or fewer) cargo is generated by each building. In boom times, 16 percent more cargo is being generated.
- **Cargo Revenues**—Not only is there more cargo in boom times, the cargo is worth more as well. Revenues per load hauled (all else being equal) are 10 percent higher (or lower), per economic level above (or below) normal.

The combination of these two makes revenue swings even more pronounced, since in boom times, you'll be generating 1.16 times more cargo at 1.2 times more revenue per load, for a total effect of:

$$1.16 \times 1.2 = 1.39 \text{ TIMES MORE REVENUE THAN NORMAL}$$

In depression, the formula is:

$$.84 \times .8 = .67 \text{ TIMES NORMAL REVENUE}$$

So your revenue potential is about twice as high in boom times as it is in a depression. Since many of your costs are relatively fixed, you can see the same railroad that made big profits in boom times start losing money at a torrential rate during a depression.

Other variables that can and should affect your strategy include:

- **Track laying**—Track laying is 10 percent more (or less) expensive for each level above (or below) normal.
- **Stock prices**—Stock prices are also 10 percent higher (or lower) for each economic level above (or below) normal. This assumes all else is equal. Since, as we've seen above, revenue and especially profits swing significantly depending on the economy, the stock price effect is usually a lot more than 10 percent.
- **Interest rates**—The prime rate runs from 5 percent in boom times to 9 percent in depression. Your credit rating will also affect the actual rate at which you can issue bonds.

In general, **when the economy is booming,** you should consider these options:

- **Add more trains**—Look around at your stations and *consider adding more trains* to haul any excess cargo piling up.
- **Refinance bonds**—Refinance any bonds you issued at high interest rates.
- **Play the stock market cautiously**—Don't get too aggressive in the stock market—you've probably made a nice profit with the rising economy, but pushing things now (especially heavy use of margin) could put you in trouble when the economy inevitably drops a bit. If the economy takes a sharp dive, it could bankrupt you.
- **Issue stock**—Conversely, now is a good time for your company to issue stock—you'll get a premium price without diluting your stock much.

When the economy is in a depression, you should consider these options:

- **Retire old trains**—To help ward off losses, this is also a good time to look through your train list and see if any of your older trains are losing money—they might be good candidates for retirement.
- **Buy stock**—If you can afford it, this is a also good time for you to buy up stock, either on the personal level or the corporate level. Prices should be low.
- **Issue Bond**—If your company has a decent credit rating, consider issuing a bond and doing a little track expansion. You can refinance the bond when the economy improves—and the track laying itself will be cheaper in a poor economy.

In an ideal world, you'd always have a booming economy. In reality, however, this won't happen, and it's best to prepare for bad times.

THE LOCAL ECONOMY

The economy as a whole is comprised of many individual industries, as depicted by the individual buildings on the map. These buildings represent entire industries native to a particular area. The industries included in the game represent some of the most common industries that relied upon railroads for transportation. Note that most of these industries had other means of transporting their goods, which are not visually depicted on the map. The primary competitor to railways for hauling large bulky goods was shipping—either using big clippers on the ocean or using barges on rivers and canals for shipping inland.

> THE INDUSTRIES CAN SURVIVE WITHOUT YOUR RAIL SERVICE, BUT IF YOU DO A GOOD JOB WITHIN A PARTICULAR AREA, YOU'LL REALLY SEE IT THRIVE, WHICH HAS LOTS OF NICE SIDE EFFECTS FOR YOUR RAILROAD—THE MOST IMPORTANT OF WHICH IS THAT MORE CARGOES ARE AVAILABLE TO HAUL.

CITY SIZE AND GROWTH

When a new map is started, the game has a target size for each city, and a target density for the areas outside the cities, called regions, which generally contain most of the mines and farms. This is largely pre-determined, as set up by the map's designer. For example, New York and London will always start out as big cities. However, there is a *random factor* built in that accounts for about 30 percent of a city's starting size—New York will always start out big, but sometimes it will start out very big, or perhaps only moderately big. In addition, the actual variety and distribution of industries is randomized, from within a set of available industries. On the Eastern U.S. map, Detroit will almost always have an auto plant, but sometimes it won't. Detroit has about a 50/50 shot of having a lumber mill. Detroit has no chance at all of having a produce orchard or a cattle yard.

Beyond the starting setup, the growth of a city or region is largely based on how well it is serviced by the rail industry. Chicago grew from a small frontier town to the third largest city in the nation in just a few decades, based largely on its role as the biggest railroad hub in the United States. Western towns that were bypassed by the railroads shriveled and died, while small towns boomed if they were serviced by multiple rail lines.

In *Railroad Tycoon II*, a city has the potential to grow to roughly 3 times its original size, if it is well served by the rail industry, with plenty of cargo hauled both into and out of the town. It won't happen instantly, but over the course of 10 to 15 years, you'll definitely see the growth. A city with no rail service will generally not disappear, but it certainly won't grow, and it will often shrink by 10 to 30 percent over the course of a decade or two.

Regions experience a bit more moderate growth, but you'll still notice it. The map's designer defines regions, and there is no way to directly detect the boundaries of a region within the game itself. However, if you load up any map in the editor, you'll see icons on the screen representing different regions, with different cargo distributions. Most maps have 10 to 20 regions defined. If you hover the mouse over one of the icons, you'll see the extent of the region.

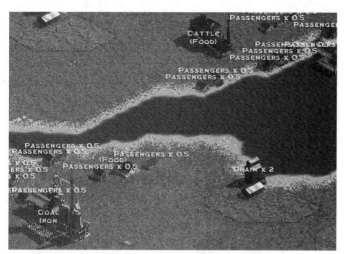

FIGURE 2-3. SUPPLY AND DEMAND OVERVIEW

SUPPLY

The product of all these industries on the map is a supply of cargoes (Figure 2-3), which will be made available for hauling from any station close enough to the industry in question. Many *buildings* produce cargo at a relatively fixed rate—an iron mine produces two loads of cargo per year. Some buildings produce cargo at a fixed rate, but that rate can be increased a bit. Farms, orchards, and livestock industries are examples of industries that produce at a set rate, but supplying them with another item can increase their rate of production.

For example, all *farms* and *orchards* (cotton, grain, sugar, produce, and coffee) receive a 50 percent production bonus to their base rate of two cargoes per year if supplied with fertilizer. One load of fertilizer is used for every two loads of crops produced, so for optimal production, supply all your farms with about one-and-a-half loads of fertilizer per year. Don't oversupply a farm if you can avoid it, it's probably better to use the excess on another farm. Similarly, the *livestock-based industries* (cattle ranch, sheep farm, and dairy farm) get a 50 percent production bonus if supplied with grain.

Finally, many *industries* produce only if supplied with raw materials (coal and iron are used by the steel mill to make steel). These industries can be particularly useful. Given one load each of iron and coal, you can generate up to six haulable loads, for three times normal profits, by properly hauling them first to a steel mill (where they are turned into steel) then hauling the two loads of steel to a tool and die factory (to become goods), then hauling the goods to a town for final sale.

Moreover, you'll generally be paid more for hauling more cargoes further along the processing chain. Hauling a load of iron is only worth a base fee of $28,000. The resulting cargo of steel will generate another $35,000 in hauling fees. The end product, goods, is worth a base fee of $42,000. The total for all three is $105,000, quite a bit more than if you'd just hauled the iron and forgotten about the rest. Of course, the base fee is only a rough guideline to what you'll actually receive. Still, the biggest profits can only be had by properly servicing most or all of the industries near your tracks.

DEMAND

The basics of demand are quite easy. Different industries demand various cargoes, as shown on the reference card included with the game. Overall demand at a station is the sum of the demand of the individual buildings encompassed within that station's radius. A special category of a "town" or a "city" is created if a station has more than four or eight houses, respectively within its radius.

Things get more interesting on the expert industrial model, thanks to the introduction of "price levels." Demand ceases to be a black or white situation. At this level, some stations have demand, but at a low price, whereas others will pay a hefty premium for some cargoes.

> TOWNS AND CITIES DEMAND A VARIETY OF CARGOES, INCLUDING PASSENGERS, MAIL, FOOD, AND GOODS. YOU CAN STILL HAUL CARGOES TO STATIONS THAT DO NOT DEMAND THEM, THOUGH YOU'LL RECEIVE ANYWHERE FROM A BIT LESS (IF YOU CHOSE THE BASIC INDUSTRIAL MODEL WHEN YOU STARTED THE GAME) TO VIRTUALLY NOTHING (IF YOU CHOSE THE EXPERT INDUSTRIAL MODEL, OR ARE PLAYING THE CAMPAIGN GAME).

CARGO PRICING

Table 2-1 shows the relationship between each cargo and the demand for it. The first column, *Cargo*, is the name of the cargo. *Base Price* shows the number of days you have to deliver the cargo before it disappears from a station. For instance, if you do not pick up mail within 300 days, it will disappear from the station (the assumption is that your customers got sick of waiting for the train and sent it by other means). *Ship Distance Base* shows the modifier applied to the base price as distance hauled increases. The higher this number is, the more you will receive for hauling that cargo across longer distances. Next, are three dates; *First Year*—the first year the cargo appears, *Cutoff for Towns*—the last date towns will accept the cargo, and *Cutoff for Cities*—the last date cities will accept the cargo. *Demand per House* shows the demand for the cargo per house in any given town or city, and the *Storage Building* column lists the station improvement that affects the cargo.

TABLE 2-1. CARGO DEMAND TABLE

Cargo	Base Price	Days to Deliver	Ship Distance	First Year	Cutoff for Towns	Cutoff for Cities	Demand per House	Storage Building
Passengers	60,000	500	0.37	1800	9999	9999	0.35	
Mail	70,000	300	0.47	1800	9999	9999	0.18	Post Office
Lumber	30,000	1,600	0.1	1800	9999	9999	0.1	
Logs	30,000	1,600	0.1	1800	0	0	0	
Milk	60,000	300	0.2	1800	1889	1889	0	Refrigerated Storage
Cattle	40,000	800	0.2	1800	0	0	0	
Steel	30,000	1,600	0.1	1800	0	0	0	
Goods	35,000	1,100	0.2	1800	9999	9999	0.2	
Autos	35,000	1,100	0.2	1900	0	9999	0.2	
Cement	35,000	1,100	0.1	1884	0	9999	0.1	
Food	50,000	600	0.2	1800	9999	9999	0.1	
Cotton	50,000	600	0.2	1800	0	0	0	Warehouse
Wool	50,000	600	0.2	1800	0	0	0	Warehouse
Paper	40,000	800	0.2	1800	0	9999	0.1	
Oil Storage	40,000	800	0.2	1860	0	1899	0.1	Liquid
Chemical Storage	40,000	800	0.2	1882	0	0	0	Liquid
Fertilizer	30,000	1,600	0.1	1905	0	0	0	
Hazardous	40,000	800	0.2	1950	0	0	0	
Coal	30,000	1,600	0.1	1800	0	1899	0.15	
Grain	30,000	1,600	0.1	1800	0	0	0	Grain Silo
Aluminum	30,000	1,600	0.1	1910	0	0	0	
Coffee	40,000	800	0.2	1800	0	0	0	Grain Silo
Tires	30,000	1,600	0.1	1900	0	0	0	
Sugar	40,000	800	0.2	1800	0	0	0	Grain Silo
Uranium	30,000	1,600	0.1	1950	0	0	0	
Pulpwood	30,000	1,600	0.1	1800	0	0	0	
Gravel	30,000	1,600	0.1	1884	0	0	0	
Iron	30,000	1,600	0.1	1800	0	0	0	

CARGO	BASE PRICE	DAYS TO DELIVER	SHIP DISTANCE	FIRST YEAR	CUTOFF FOR TOWNS	CUTOFF FOR CITIES	DEMAND PER HOUSE	STORAGE BUILDING
Produce	30,000	1,600	0.1	1800	0	0	0	Refrigerated Storage
Bauxite	30,000	1,600	0.1	1800	0	0	0	
Diesel	30,000	1,600	0.1	1890	0	0	0	
Rubber	30,000	1,600	0.1	1900	0	0	0	
Dining	0	0	0.0	1846	0	0	0	
Caboose	0	0	0.0	1839	0	0	0	

Cargo pricing starts with the base value listed in the chart. It is modified for distance hauled and time to deliver according to the factors mentioned above. If cargo is hauled to a station that doesn't demand it, only a fractional price will be paid, depending on the industrial model setting for the scenario—the one you chose when starting the scenario. The prices for cargo not in demand are 80 percent, 50 percent, and 30 percent of full price, respectively, depending on whether the player is at the *Easy*, *Medium* or *Hard* industry model. If the cargo is in demand, 100 percent is paid, unless the industry model is *Expert*, in which case demand levels kick in as shown in Table 2-2. Demand levels are based on the number of houses or industries in the area demanding the cargo, and how much of that cargo they have received recently. If they receive a lot of cargo, demand falls off. The maximum demand level is 9, and the minimum is 0. There's almost a threefold price swing between the highest and lowest level, so this is an important item.

TABLE 2-2. PERCENTAGE OF FULL PRICE PAID BASED UPON DEMAND LEVEL

PERCENTAGE OF FULL PRICE	DEMAND LEVEL
50%	0
60%	1
70%	2
80%	3
90%	4
100%	5
110%	6
120%	7
130%	8
140%	9

Price levels range from zero (0) to nine (9). A price level of zero for a particular cargo is still better than no demand at all, it just means that price level is as low as it will go for any station that demands a cargo.

Basically, the price level depends on how badly the cargo is needed at that station. This depends on the number and type of industries demanding the cargo, and how much of that cargo they've received recently. If more than one industry at a station demand the cargo, the price level will usually be higher, and will be slower to drop and faster to rebound if a large delivery is made.

There are several other things that can bump up cargo revenues. Many station buildings bump up passenger revenue, as does a dining car. A train that has set a speed record gets a 15 percent bonus on passenger revenue. Various manager bonuses can also increase cargo revenues.

If, for a particular run, your train travels over tracks or to or from a station that doesn't belong to you, you have to pay the owner a chunk of the revenue. The owner will not contribute to the fuel or train costs, so you have to keep the portion of the revenue you're paying down or you can lose money on a run.

If you don't own the origination station, you have to pay a fee of $1,000 per cargo hauled to its owner—a full, six-car train will pay $6,000. If you don't own the destination station, you also have to pay $1,000 per cargo, plus give up any station bonuses (restaurant, hotel and saloon bonuses to passenger revenue) to the owner.

If you don't own all the track, then the non-station revenue (total revenue minus the above amounts) is split, according to the percentage of track upon which the route was run. If your train hauls 3 loads of coal 20 squares, of which 16 are yours and 4 belong to the Union Pacific (UP), for a total run of $106,000, then the non-station revenue is $100,000 (excluding the $6,000 in station fees). You get 16/20 or 80 percent of the non-station revenue ($80,000). The UP gets $20,000. If you own both stations, you also get to keep the $6,000 in station fees. Note that the UP does not have to eat a portion of your train's fuel or maintenance costs.

> TO MAKE THE BIGGEST PROFITS, SPREAD YOUR DELIVERIES OUT. INSTEAD OF DUMPING ALL YOUR GRAIN INTO A SINGLE STATION WITH ONE BAKERY, DISTRIBUTE TO MULTIPLE STATIONS WITH NEARBY BAKERIES, OR TO A STATION LOCATED NEAR SEVERAL BAKERIES.

FREIGHT REVENUE 101

TO DETERMINE THE BEST RETURN FOR LOADS HAULED, PLEASE REFER TO THE CHARTS IN APPENDIX A AND USE THESE GENERAL RULES OF THUMB:

- SLOW DELIVERIES EQUAL LESS MONEY.
- GIVEN THE BENEFITS OF THE MODIFYING STORAGE BUILDINGS, THE LONGER YOU HAUL A PERISHABLE CARGO, THE MORE TIME YOU ARE GIVEN.
- THE LATER THE DATE, THE ROT FACTOR IS INCREASED AS TRAINS BECOME FASTER.
- SOME CARGOES ARE MORE TIME SENSITIVE THAN OTHERS ARE. THESE RATES CAN BE CHECKED IN THE "DAYS TO BE DELIVERED" COLUMN ON THE REFERENCE CARD OR BY RIGHT-CLICKING ON A CARGO TO SEE THE BASIC DELIVERY TIME YOU HAVE.

BUYING INDUSTRIES

The ability to buy industries opens a lot of new possibilities, but is only available on the expert industrial model. In general, by buying up the most profitable industries you're servicing, you'll be able to significantly increase your profits, and often turn a marginal line into a profitable one, with industrial profits making up for lackluster hauling revenues.

You can buy any industry on the map except housing. Click on an industry to see how profitable it is, and how much it costs. Industry profitability is determined by how many loads are delivered to and picked up from an industry. To count towards profitability, a picked-up load must be delivered to another station that demands it. Profitability is based on a running average of the last few years, so if an industry is ignored for a year, it does not immediately plunge into heavy losses. As you start to service an industry, you'll often see a profitability increase over several years from merely "good" to the optimal "gushing cash." The actual dollar profit of an industry is based on its purchase price—a steel mill (cost $800,000) rated as "gushing cash" will usually be making about four times as much as a cotton farm (cost $200,000). In general, you want to buy only industries rated "lucrative", "very lucrative", or "gushing cash". An industry rated as "gushing cash" will usually make an annual return of 20 percent or more on its purchase price (about $160,000 for a steel mill).

ONE DOWNSIDE TO BUYING INDUSTRIES IS THAT IT ENCOURAGES YOU TO OVERSUPPLY THE STATIONS AT WHICH YOU OWN INDUSTRIES— TRADING HAULING PROFITS FOR INDUSTRY PROFITS. AS A GENERAL RULE OF THUMB, IF YOU CAN EASILY DISTRIBUTE YOUR CARGO TO THREE OR MORE INDUSTRIES THAT DEMAND IT, DO SO, KEEPING PRICE LEVELS HIGH, BUT PROBABLY HOLDING DOWN INDUSTRY PROFITS BELOW A LEVEL WHERE YOU'D BE INCLINED TO BUY THEM. IF YOU'RE FORCED TO HAUL TO ONLY THE ONE OR TWO INDUSTRIES THAT DEMAND YOUR CARGOES, DO SO, SUFFER THE LOW PRICE LEVEL, BUT BE PREPARED TO BUY UP THOSE INDUSTRIES AS THEIR PROFITS RISE. IF YOU'RE PLAYING AGAINST AI OPPONENTS, YOU MIGHT WANT TO BUY THE INDUSTRIES BEFORE THEY BECOME LUCRATIVE, TO PREVENT THE AI FROM BUYING THEM OUT FROM UNDER YOU.

BONUSES

THERE ARE A NUMBER OF BONUSES TO BE AWARDED AND EARNED THROUGHOUT THE GAME. THEY ALL VARY FROM HARD-SET PERCENTAGES TO RANDOM EVENT-DRIVEN BONUSES, INCLUDING:

· COMPANY MANAGERS CAN ADD A PERCENTAGE OF ADDED VALUE TO CERTAIN CARGO. FOR EXAMPLE, ANDREW CARNEGIE PRODUCES A BIG REVENUE BONUS FOR STEEL FOR ANY COMPANY HE MANAGES.

· EVENT-DRIVEN BONUSES OCCUR THROUGHOUT THE GAME SUCH AS A COAL STRIKE RAISING THE PRICE OF COAL HAULS OR A CITY ANNOUNCING AN INCENTIVE BONUS FOR CONNECTING TO IT.

· DINING CARS ATTACHED TO AT LEAST ONE OTHER PASSENGER CAR INCREASE THE VALUE OF THAT HAUL BY 20 PERCENT.

· RECORD-SETTING TRAINS, IF HAULING PASSENGERS, INCREASE THAT HAUL'S VALUE BY 15 PERCENT.

· CURRENT ECONOMIC STATES, SUCH AS "BOOM TIMES" WILL INCUR BONUSES OF 20 PERCENT.

· LARGE RESTAURANTS, SMALL RESTAURANTS, LARGE HOTELS, SMALL HOTELS, AND SALOONS WILL BRING BONUSES OF 30 PERCENT, 20 PERCENT, 40 PERCENT, 20 PERCENT, AND 10 PERCENT, RESPECTIVELY.

PART II

Men, Machines, and Industries

A SOLID UNDERSTANDING OF THE ECONOMICS OF THE GAME—AND SOME BASIC STRATEGIES WILL ONLY GET YOU SO FAR—SHOWS THAT THERE ARE OTHER FACTORS THAT DIRECTLY IMPACT YOUR ABILITY TO MANAGE YOUR FLEDGLING IRON EMPIRE. THIS SECTION COVERS THE TYCOONS, MANAGERS, AND INDUSTRIES OF *RAILROAD TYCOON II*, GIVING YOU INFORMATION AND STRATEGIES FOR BEATING THEM, USING THEM, AND MAXIMIZING THEIR STRENGTHS RESPECTIVELY.

Of Railroad Barons and Robbers

IF YOU'RE LIKE MOST PLAYERS, YOU ORIGINALLY THOUGHT THAT THE COMPUTER PLAYERS—THE TYCOONS YOU FACE IN THE GAME—ARE PRETTY MUCH THE SAME. HOWEVER, IF YOU'VE PLAYED THROUGH A FEW OF THE SCENARIOS, YOU'VE DISCOVERED THAT THEIR STYLES ARE VERY DIFFERENT, MAKING THEM CHALLENGING OPPONENTS. LIKEWISE, YOU MAY HAVE NOTICED THE DIFFERENCES IN MANAGER BONUSES, BUT YOU PROBABLY HAVEN'T TAKEN COMPLETE ADVANTAGE OF THEM. THIS SECTION GIVES YOU SOME DIRT ON EACH TYCOON AND MANAGER THAT YOU'LL FIND USEFUL WHENEVER YOU GO HEAD-TO-HEAD WITH THEM, OR WHENEVER YOU LOOK TO HIRE A PARTICULAR MANAGER.

THE CHAIRMEN

Each chairman has unique tendencies that are, for the most part, based upon their historical actions. For instance, don't expect Jay Gould—a stockbroker by trade—to back out of your company's stock for any reason—he'll hold on like a pit bull through just about every trick you throw at him, while he does his best to undermine you. Likewise, don't expect Mr. Gould to start his own company—he'd rather mess with yours. When he shows up in the opponent list, it's going to get nasty in a hurry.

Table 3-1 lists the inclinations of the tycoons when they're played by the AI. Here's how to read the seven categories:

- *Starts Company*—Higher number means they'll start a company earlier in the face of more competition
- *Margin Buying*—Higher number is more inclined to use margin, if available
- *Short Selling*—Higher number is more inclined to short sell stocks, if available
- *Investing in Others*—Higher number is more inclined to invest in companies other than their own (such as perhaps your company)
- *Issue Bonds*—Higher number will more readily issue bonds with their company, for expansion and other purposes.
- *Expand Rail*—Higher number will expand track faster and to more far flung places.
- *Industry Investment*—Higher number will buy more buildings on the map.

When interpreting the table, 100 is average and 200 is maximum. A tycoon with a below average number in a given column is very unlikely to focus on that strategy while a tycoon with a 200 score in a column will *always* focus on that strategy. Numbers below 100 are rarely acted upon unless following that tactic yields a very obvious successful outcome.

TABLE 3-1. TYCOON TENDENCIES

NAME	STARTS COMPANY	MARGIN BUYING	SHORT SELLING	INVESTING IN OTHERS	ISSUE BONDS	EXPAND RAIL	INDUSTRY INVESTMENT
Attlee, Clement	35	100	100	50	145	100	135
Bismarck, Otto von	20	100	100	120	150	30	175
Bleichroder, Gerson von	50	75	55	150	100	40	175
Brunel, Isambard Kingdom	200	25	25	100	175	200	80
Crocker, Charles	200	100	10	200	100	200	135
Donnersmarck, Henckel von	100	115	125	180	105	90	145
Drew, Daniel	140	180	180	150	85	100	35
Durant, Thomas	100	115	100	100	175	100	165
Emperor Meiji	140	100	100	100	100	100	100
Fisk, James	170	185	145	165	100	100	160

NAME	STARTS COMPANY	MARGIN BUYING	SHORT SELLING	INVESTING IN OTHERS	ISSUE BONDS	EXPAND RAIL	INDUSTRY INVESTMENT
Fleming, Sir Sanford	100	100	100	120	200	100	20
Forrest, Sir John	125	85	75	100	140	175	40
Fremont, John C.	180	70	70	60	170	135	100
General Gentaro	25	30	30	100	100	180	100
Gould, Jay	20	200	200	200	90	55	110
Hansemann, Adolph von	45	200	100	155	100	65	150
Harriman, Edward Henry	170	185	190	160	120	180	185
Hill, James	200	100	100	50	200	200	140
Hincks, Sir Francis	100	100	100	100	100	120	75
Holliday, Cyrus K.	165	40	35	100	125	135	100
Hopkins, Mark	100	100	100	100	100	100	100
Hudson, George	135	200	200	120	140	70	100
Huntington, Collis	190	70	70	105	155	120	170
Jay Cooke,	80	115	100	150	200	100	100
Kai-Shek, Chiang	145	120	115	120	20	55	100
Keith, Minor	130	100	100	155	100	120	175
Morgan, J.P.	100	130	100	200	100	100	200
Napoleon III	100	100	100	100	100	145	160
Nehru, Jawaharlal	35	100	100	35	100	165	145
Platner, George	140	100	100	100	115	165	100
Rhodes, Cecil	200	100	100	100	100	200	155
Scott, Thomas	130	100	100	100	145	170	100
Stanford, Leland	100	100	40	185	120	100	140
Stephen, Sir George	100	100	100	100	100	100	50
Strathconda, Lord	100	100	100	100	100	100	20
Thomas, Philip E.	100	100	100	100	100	100	100
Train, George F.	160	100	100	100	100	100	200
Vanderbilt, Cornelius	100	100	100	100	100	100	190
Wheelwright, William	120	120	80	100	100	115	170
Zedong, Mao	20	20	20	100	140	145	100

Since these tendencies can be combined in many ways, and none are absolute guarantees of the AI's behavior in every situation, it's best to think of these in general terms, or better, general tycoon types:

- **Expansionist (Company Starts/Expand Rail)** — Because *Railroad Tycoon II* does not exclude multiple stations in a service area, an aggressive expansion by the computer will not necessarily exclude you from important regions. This will give the expansionist first dibs on optimal station placement but not exclusive rights to the resources there. This means the player who provides the most comprehensive service (material delivery and pick up) will get the cargo. This leads to natural competition for cargo without using an artificial rate war. The longer you have a train wait for cargo the lower the rate earned due to maintenance costs and lost opportunity.

- **Stock Market Wrangler (Investing in Others/Margin Buying/Short Selling)** — Since some scenarios rely on personal net worth, an aggressive stock manipulator can be particularly difficult to deal with. It is best not to delay in acquiring at least some of such an opponent's stock. Later in the game it may be all but impossible to dig them out. Also, the same will hold true for your own stock. Keep as much of your stock in your own hands when playing such an opponent—this goes for human opponents too!

- **Centralist (Industry Investments/Issue Bonds)** — Because the centralist doesn't usually "dabble" in the stock market heavily, they usually become well entrenched in their own stock and rapidly buy up industries that they will service with their railroad. They also have the annoying habit of buying profitable industries you are servicing. If an industry you are servicing is gushing cash or very lucrative, and you don't own it, then this type will likely buy it up in a single heartbeat.

> THE AI CAN PURCHASE NEWLY ISSUED STOCK AT THE SPEED OF THE COMPUTER. IN OTHER WORDS, IT WILL SEEM LIKE IT'S BUYING STOCK WHEN NONE APPEARS TO BE AVAILABLE. TO HAVE A FIGHTING CHANCE, PRESS PAUSE BEFORE YOU ENTER THE STOCK MARKET OR ISSUE STOCK YOU WISH TO PURCHASE YOURSELF.

THE MANAGERS

Okay, there's one important point here to remember! These managers don't carry grudges so use them like tools! Really, they like it. If you need to build a lot of track and Robert Stevens shows up at your company door looking for work, hire him, it usually pays. When that phase of your work is done, you can fire him and get someone who is suited to help you with the next phase of your work.

Managers also can figure into winning strategies in the campaign. Results vary, but you can always see where you're losing money. You should see if a particular manager is available to plug that hole. Lowering your diesel engine purchase costs by 30 percent can go a very long way in the "Dilemma Down Under" scenario. Also artificially lowering your own stock price with a manager is a great way to buy into your own company and make a sudden profit when you fire that manager.

The managers perform tasks that can both improve and hinder your performance; however, unlike in the real world, there are no managers in *Railroad Tycoon II* that don't have a single useful function.

Each manager must be paid a monthly *salary* in exchange for his bonus. No manager will have more than four bonuses; however, not all managers are equally skilled when it comes to money management and purchases. Pick the right manager for the job that needs to be done, and use your manager's skills to your advantage as you are in control of that manager's employment. Table 3-2 lists each manager's salary and explains each bonus.

STEEL
WATER
TOWER

SCAFFOLDING
STYLE LEGS

TABLE 3-2. THE MANAGERS

NAME	SALARY	BONUS 1	BONUS 2	BONUS 3	BONUS 4
Albert A. Robinson	19,000	Track building -15%	Stock Price 10% lower		
Allen Mac Nab	10,000	Company Overhead -10%	Goodwill +10%		
Ames Oakes	8,000	Engine Purchase +12%	Credit Rating +1 level	Goodwill +10%	Station Building -10%
Andre Chapelon	36,000	All Engine Speed +10%			
Andrew Carnegie	52,000	Bridge Building -30%	Station Building -15%	Steel Revenue +10%	
Bat Masterson	38,000	Train Safety +50%	Passenger Revenue +5%	Station Revenue +5%	
Ben Holladay	26,000	Company Overhead -15%	Mail Revenue +10%		
Charles F. Mayer	89,000	Bridge Building -20%	Track Building -40%		
Charles M. Hayes	77,000	Company Overhead -5%	Track Building -40%	Train Safety -5%	
Daniel Gooch	44,000	Company Overhead -5%	All Engine Purchase -20%	Track Building -5%	Iron Revenue +20%
Daniel Willard	10,000	All Fuel -10%			
Dr. Robert Garbe	6,000	Steam Engine Purchase -15%			
Dr. Wilhelm Schmidt	22,000	All Fuel -10%	Steam Traction +10%		
Ernst Siemens	6,000	Electric Engine Purchase -30%			
Eugen V. Debs	65,000	Company Overhead +25%	Goodwill +5%	Train Safety +25%	Passenger Revenue +10%
Fredrick Billings	3,000	Company Overhead -10%			

Name	Salary	Bonus 1	Bonus 2	Bonus 3	Bonus 4
George Nagelmachers	46,000	Car Maintenance +10%	Passenger Revenue +15%		
George Pullman	94,000	Car Maintenance +20%	Passenger Revenue +25%	Station Revenue +5%	
George Stephenson	43,000	All Engine Purchase -25%	Passenger Revenue +5%		
George Westinghouse	29,000	Car Maintenance +5%	Train Safety +25%	Passenger Revenue +5%	
Ginery Twitchell	4,000	Stock Price -15%	Goodwill +15%		
Henri Giffard	20,000	Company Overhead +20%	Engine Maintenance -10%	Steam Engine Speed +5%	
Henry Booth	13,000	Car Maintenance -10%			
Herbert Garratt	14,000	Steam Fuel Costs -40%	All Engine Speed -5%		
John Wootten	4,000	Engine Maintenance +10%	All Engine Fuel -5%	Steam Engine Fuel -25%	
John Work Garrett	21,000	Track Building Cost -5%	Electric Track Building -40%	Track Grade Building -20%	
Johns Hopkins	41,000	Passenger Revenue +10%			
Oscar G. Murray	87,000	Station Turnaround Time 20% Faster	All Cargo Revenue +5%		
Philip Randolph	29,000	Company Overhead +40%	Train Safety +10%	Passenger Revenue +10%	
Richard Trevithick	14,000	All Engine Purchase -15%	All Engine Maintenance +15%	All Engine Speed +10	
Robert Gerwig	37,000	Bridge Building -40%	Track Building on Grade -50%	Electric Engine Acceleration +10%	

TABLE 3-2. THE MANAGERS (continued)

NAME	SALARY	BONUS 1	BONUS 2	BONUS 3	BONUS 4
Robert Stevens	73,000	All Track Building -25%	Track Maintenance -10%		
Roy B. White	12,000	Station Building -20%	Track Building +15%	Station Turnaround Time 20% Faster	
Rudolph Diesel	3,000	Diesel Engine Purchase -25%	Stock Prices -10%		
Theodore D. Judah	29,000	Company Overhead -30%	Track Building -15%		
Thomas Crampton	4,000	Track Maintenance +10%	All Engine Acceleration +10%	Steam Engine Speed +15%	
Thomas Swann	6,000	Goodwill +10%			
William C. VanHorne	26,000	Station Building -10%	Track Building -15%	Track Building on Grade -20%	Electric Engine Fuel -10%
William J. Palmer	39,000	Track Building -10%	Coal Revenue +30%		
William Strong	11,000	Company Overhead +20%	Station Building -10%	Station Revenue 5%	

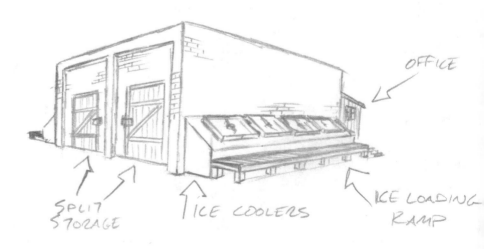

SPLIT STORAGE

ICE COOLERS

OFFICE

ICE LOADING RAMP

MEN, MACHINES, AND INDUSTRIES

4

The Trains

WITH 60 LOCOMOTIVES TO CHOOSE FROM,

YOU NEED TO PICK YOUR ENGINES CAREFULLY.

IT'S BEST TO SELECT A TRAIN BASED ON ALL

THE REQUIREMENTS FOR THE RUN YOU HAVE IN

MIND. WHILE A GENERAL APPROACH MAY APPLY

AT TIMES, TO GET THE BEST RESULTS YOU'LL

NEED TO GET THE RIGHT LOCOMOTIVE FOR THE

JOB. THIS CHAPTER GIVES YOU ALL OF THE

INFORMATION YOU'LL NEED TO MAKE AN

INFORMED CHOICE.

WORKHORSES OF THE IRON HIGHWAY

Your railroad won't get very far without careful selection, management, and maintenance of trains. *Railroad Tycoon II* spans roughly 200 years, and in each time period, you'll be able to select various trains to get the job done. Before taking a look at some of the more useful engines in the game, let's take a look at some of the factors that affect trains and their operation in *Railroad Tycoon II*.

PURCHASING FACTORS

When you decide to purchase a train in Railroad Tycoon II, the Purchase dialog provides crucial information about each train that is currently available. It's important to choose carefully, especially when money is tight. You'll have to live with the choices you make, so take the time to analyze your purchase before making it:

- **Cost**—This is the price of the train you are analyzing. It's important to know that the most expensive train you can buy is *not* always the best train to buy. Look at all other factors first, *then* take a look at cost as the final determining factor.

- **Maintenance**—This is the cost of keeping the train running during the course of a year. Every train has a maintenance cost associated with it, so the important thing here is to weigh this factor against the pros and cons of other trains available. A train with a high maintenance cost may make sense, given good numbers in its other attributes.

- **Fuel**—This line gives you the fuel type and cost for each locomotive. As with maintenance, every train has this cost associated with it, so do some comparisons based upon the other factors first. If, however, a train's fuel cost is out of line, select another

train, provided its capabilities are similar. Note that the fuel cost shown is an estimate, and takes distance traveled into account. Faster trains will tend to use more fuel, since they travel further per year.

- **Acceleration**—This is a measure of how fast a train will get out of the station and up to top speed. This is important for short routes—if a train has poor (or worse) acceleration, it may never reach top speed before reaching its destination, and you should factor that into your top speed calculations. Also, on heavily traveled routes trains will tend to stop more to let other trains by, especially if the route has only single track.

- **Reliability**—This is usually the most important factor. If a train is less reliable, breakdowns will occur more often. Be conscious of your connections and the terrain, and try not to choose trains with poor or worse reliability ratings. Also, be more wary of poor reliability on a train that will be on your main line. A blockage on a heavily traveled main line is far worse than one on a spur to a few coal mines.

- **Top Speed**—Examine this chart carefully. By default, it shows a train's top speed when hauling a certain number of 40-ton cars over variable grades. You can change the tonnage to see correspondingly different numbers in the chart. Pay special attention to this chart if you're purchasing a train for a hilly route. However, since you run the whole show, you should minimize poor performance on grades by working to build your track as flat as possible.

STATIONS

Stations are not merely places where trains pick up and deliver cargo. They serve an important role in train maintenance and performance. Within a station, you can—better, you *must*—add upgrades that will make your trains perform better, and keep breakdowns to a minimum. It's important to note that a train must merely pass through a station with these upgrades—the train doesn't have to stop there—for them to have effect:

- **Roundhouse**—The roundhouse performs necessary maintenance on trains. A train's oil level is the proxy for how recently it has received maintenance. Trains with less oil run a higher breakdown risk. If your train completely runs out of oil, breakdown risk triples, and maintenance costs go way up, too. If you're continually running low on oil, add roundhouses along your routes to keep oil levels high.

- **Water Tower**—Crucial for all steam engines, the water tower enables trains to generate steam. Low water levels will mean that a train can't move as fast—in fact, in many cases they will take years to limp to their destinations without water. There is no adverse effect until the train runs completely out of water.

- **Sanding Tower**—Sand is added to trains to improve performance over steep grades. Without sand, the train's wheels can't generate traction, and the effect of the grade is doubled — so a 2% grade acts like a 4% grade. There is no adverse effect until the train runs completely out of sand.

The longer it is between stations with these upgrades, the more likely it is that trains will have problems. In general, you'll want a water tower every 30 squares or so along a line. Sanding tower placement depends on how steep the grades are where you're building. In a hilly area, you may want sanding towers every 10 squares (even going so far as to place a small station along the track for no reason other than to add sand). In flat areas, you can place sanding towers 50 or even 100 squares apart. Finally, the effect of roundhouses lasts the longest — trains can go 100 squares or more between visits. However, due to their high costs, be conservative with roundhouses initially. As traffic increases, you may want more roundhouses than absolutely necessary, to keep oil levels high and breakdown frequency down.

CARGO

A train's cargo, or consist, has everything to do with how it will perform. Additional cars add tonnage to a train's consist, and based upon engine capabilities, can severely impact a train's ability to perform.

When you purchase a train, pay close attention to the Top Speed chart in the Purchase dialog box. If your route is over a flat grade, then familiarize yourself with the engine's 0-2 percent numbers. However, don't make the mistake of thinking that a train with good numbers in this area will do all right when grades hit 4 to 6 percent. There is a marked decrease in performance when trains hit this type of terrain.

Also, note that the number of cars is a huge factor. Don't overload your trains with multiple cars. They won't get to their destinations fast enough to help you, and you'll increase the chances that they'll breakdown. This is especially true of trains before 1850—be very careful with these older trains and keep them on the light side to avoid problems.

IN HIGH CRIME AREAS (SUCH AS THE WESTERN U.S. IN THE LATE 1800S), ADD A CABOOSE TO REDUCE ROBBERIES. IF ROBBERIES AREN'T A PROBLEM, THEN A CABOOSE BECOMES OF MARGINAL VALUE, REDUCING BREAKDOWNS BY 25 PERCENTAGE, BUT ADDING WEIGHT AND LENGTH TO YOUR TRAIN.

BREAKDOWNS AND CRASHES

Unfortunately, even the most careful selection of trains, regular maintenance in stations, and careful cargo selection won't be able to keep your trains from occasionally breaking down or crashing.

When a train breaks down, it will stop for awhile, preventing any train from passing it. Your company's goodwill will be hurt, and the train in question, as well as those stacked up behind it, will take a lot longer to reach their destination.

The likelihood of any given train breaking down is calculated based upon several factors, but they all begin with a train's reliability rating. Table 4-1 lists some of the variables that determine the odds of train breakdowns and crashes. The reliability rating is found in each train's Purchase dialog, and "Cells Traveled Between Breakdowns" is a portion of the calculation used to determine whether or not a train will break down over time.

Beyond these set breakdown rates, there are additional variables in the likelihood of a breakdown or crash:

- **Oil Level**—If you're out of oil, breakdown odds triple. If oil level is one notch above empty, breakdown odds are double. At the half full level, the breakdown odds are 50 percent higher than normal.

- **Throttle**—Normal throttle setting is just below the red line, or 85 percent of maximum power. At maximum power, the normal breakdown rate is quadrupled.

TABLE 4-1. TRAIN CRASH ODDS

TRAIN RATING RELIABILITY	CELLS TRAVELED BETWEEN BREAKDOWNS (AVERAGE)
Atrocious	400
Extremely Poor	600
Very Poor	875
Poor	1,100
Below Average	1,400
Average	1,800
Above Average	2,500
Good	4,000
Very Good	6,000
Outstanding	12,000
Near Perfect	24,000

- **Weight Hauled**—The first 50 tons hauled are free. Every additional 200 tons hauled doubles the breakdown odds. For heavy freight haulers, pay particular attention to reliability.

- **Grade**—For every 2 percent grade climbed, weight is roughly quadrupled. For example, a train hauling 120 tons up a 2% grade is effectively hauling about 480 tons—roughly quadrupling normal breakdown odds.

- **Engine Age**—After 2 years, the odds of breakdown rise steadily. A 10-year-old train is 33 percent more likely to break down. A 20-year-old train is 66 percent more likely to break down.

- **Caboose**—A caboose reduces breakdown odds by 25 percent.

Crashes are extreme breakdown cases. Once the computer has randomly determined that your trains will breakdown or crash, there is a straight 20 percent chance of it crashing and an 80 percent chance of it having a breakdown.

With all this in mind, a few clear strategies will help you get the most from your trains:

- **Use reliable trains for the mountains**. The steep grades will greatly increase breakdown percentages, so make sure you've chosen a train with the highest reliability possible for these routes.

- **Push the throttle on brand new trains, but not older ones**. The breakdown percentage is manageable on new trains at full throttle, but add the age factor and you might have as much as a 100 percent chance of a breakdown!

- **Replace trains after 10 to 20 years of service**. Old trains will break down more often—replace them early to keep things rolling along.

- **Never let trains run out of oil.** If you're experiencing an extraordinary amount of breakdowns, place more roundhouses on your route to keep the oil levels near their maximum.

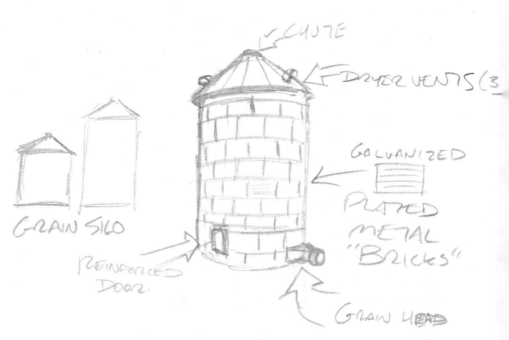

THE CREAM OF THE CROP

While statistics can tell you generally what an engine is capable of accomplishing, most engines are very particular and only the engineer and mechanics can tell you what it can really do. However, we'll highlight a few of the best for certain time periods and/or special uses, particularly in *Railroad Tycoon II*. For more statistics on these trains, see Appendix B.

1800-1849

THE JOHN BULL 2-4-0 (1831)

DESCRIPTION:	The John Bull was a modification of an English design that was also the first to use a "cow catcher" among its many customizations. It was shipped to the United States in pieces and was assembled by an engineer who had never seen a locomotive before—he added the cow catcher, headlight, and other enhancements. The original John Bull stayed in service till about 1849. It was the first locomotive saved as a national relic in the United States.
USAGE:	Its top speed on level track and its slightly better reliability make it a generally better passenger mover when passengers pay well. If you use only two cars in your consist you'll get it's best performance.

THE AMERICAN 4-4-0 (1848)

DESCRIPTION: The name "American" came from the description of this general configuration as being the American Standard engine type. By 1870, 85 percent of all U.S. locomotives where of this type. Varieties of this type of engine where used well into the 1900's and are etched into railroading history.

USAGE: The American is an inexpensive and versatile locomotive. Its high flat land speed combined with higher reliability will not be match for 20 years when another variant, the Eight Wheeler, becomes available. This is the first locomotive you can work hard without it constantly blowing up in your. The throttle can be used with some caution with this locomotive.

1850-1899

THE CONSOLIDATION 2-8-0 (1877)

2-8-0 CONSOLIDATION						
COST:				$51,000		
MAINTENANCE:				$8,000 / YEAR		
FUEL (STEAM):				$19,512 / YEAR		
ACCELERATION:				BELOW AVERAGE		
RELIABILITY:				GOOD		

	TOP SPEED (MPH)					
	CARS @ 30 TONS EACH					
	1	2	3	4	5	6
GRADE 0%	40	38	36	33	31	29
2%	32	27	23	20	17	15
4%	20	15	11	8	6	4
6%	10	5	3	2	1	1

DESCRIPTION: Surprisingly, the Consolidation took some time to gain general acceptance after its early creation in 1866. However, once it did it became a mainstay on many freight lines for years and was used till the end of the steam era.

USAGE: Its high reliability, reasonable speed, and good load hauling make it a good freighter. In a pinch, it's a respectable express locomotive but there are others in this time frame that fit that role better.

THE THREE-TRUCK SHAY (1882)

DESCRIPTION: The Three-Truck Shay was the first geared locomotive. Designed to haul wood from hilly and generally inaccessible regions, the Shay could scale 14 percent grades. At one time or another, versions were created that burned wood, coal, and oil.

USAGE: This is a truly special use locomotive. Its poor flat grade speed makes it useless in anything but difficult terrain; high grades are where this locomotive shines. Also, its good reliability keeps the need for frequent repair stops to a minimum.

THE MOGUL 2-6-0 (1895)

DESCRIPTION: While the wheel configuration had been around for a number of years it wasn't officially called the Mogul until 1872. Built until the 1930's, it became a prime example of dependable, all-purpose locomotive power in the late 1800's.

USAGE: Good speed and good pulling power make this an excellent replacement for the Consolidation. Although your operation costs will go up about 25 percent, the improvements will show up in the bottom line.

1900-1929

THE PACIFIC 4-6-2 (1908)

DESCRIPTION:	This wheel configuration turned out to be one of the fastest steam designs produced. Often modified later in life for other uses, the Pacific was the standard passenger locomotive for many railways around the world.
USAGE:	The Pacific was the first of the true high-speed locomotives. Don't expect this engine to pull much, but if you need to move perishable items or fussy passengers this will do it quickly. Its speed will often compensate for a slightly lower dependability rate. Also, this is *not* a mountain train, so avoid it in the "Whistle Stops and Promises" campaign if you want the Gold.

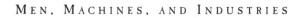

THE MIKADO 2-8-2 (1919)

| | DESCRIPTION: | The first Mikados were built in 1897 for the narrow-gauge railroad in Japan—hence the moniker. The train's performance earned it a great reputation, and it was produced and distributed widely throughout the world. |
| | USAGE: | This locomotive has power to spare. Though its top speed is not tremendous, its pulling power gives it great range. It also has the first decent acceleration for a freight engine, and its reliability makes the initial purchase cost seem barely a consideration. The "Which Way to the Coast?" campaign is a prime proving ground for this locomotive's abilities. |

THE CLASS B12 4-6-0 (1923)

	DESCRIPTION:	A version of this class was named the Flying Scotsman and ran express passenger service from London, England, to Edinburgh, Scotland, till 1963.
	USAGE:	Although its initial cost is a bit steep, this is a very fine locomotive. Its high speed can be maintained at lower grades, and it can still climb steep slopes for very short distances. This locomotive is the last of the golden age steam engines. The competition for top locomotives really heats up from here on.

1930-1949

THE GG-1 (1935)

DESCRIPTION: The GG-1 became a pet project for famed U.S. industrial designer Raymond Lowey. Through his inspiration, the GG-1's entire body was welded instead of riveted. This fact as well as its no-nonsense design gave it a distinct look. The GG-1 proved not only stylish, but extremely versatile. Able to run at high speeds and with very heavy loads, the GG-1 introduced the power of electric locomotives to the United States. The GG-1 was in service till 1983 and was the last survivor of Lowey-inspired locomotives.

Usage: If you can afford the electrical outlay, the GG-1 will make you glad you did. High speeds and great hauling power will pay for it's initial cost in short order. The GG-1 has the highest reliability rating of any locomotive in *Railroad Tycoon II*.

THE CLASS E 18 (1936)

DESCRIPTION:	The design of the Class E 18 was the winner of the 1933 electric express locomotive development trials in Germany. Over 50 were built up to 1945 and were still in service until 1984. Capable of high speed, it could also be used for a variety of freight jobs.
USAGE:	This is another great electric locomotive. Half the cost of most engines available at this time, the E 18's performance is equal to most locomotives throughout its life span. Its good reliability and fast acceleration make it a great buy.

54

THE F9 (1949)

DESCRIPTION:	The F9 is a natural progression from the F3 and F7 from the point of view of design. Although the body type is barely distinguishable from its earlier predecessor (the F7) by all but the most dedicated rail fans, the increased power and performance helped prove that diesels where here to stay. Success of diesels like these helped push back the growing interest in electrification in many countries.
USAGE:	It's very fast, and it maintains that speed through a great range of grades. You'll find that the initial cost is a bit overbearing; but like many of the later locomotives you'll find that it can do the work of any two locomotives before 1900. Buy now, thank me later.

> THE PRICES OF THESE LOCOMOTIVES
> DURING THIS TIME PERIOD ARE SO
> HIGH, A KEEN EYE SHOULD BE
> PLACED ON RELIABILITY. THE LOSS OF
> JUST ONE LOCOMOTIVE CAN KILL
> YOUR LINE IF IT HAPPENS AT THE
> WRONG TIME.

1950-2008

THE V200 (1959)

DESCRIPTION:	Production of the V200 began in 1956. However, it didn't reach its load-hauling potential until 1960, when track improvements in Germany enabled it to run at greater speeds and distances. The use of a diesel-hydraulic transmission, good body design, and lightweight bogies kept the weight down, allowing the V200 to have one of the best power-to-weight ratios of its time.
USAGE:	This is a tough call for the time period; however, all things considered this is a fine machine and should not be overlooked. Where electrification is not possible and money is tight, the V200 will give you the best bang for the buck. Consider using cabooses whenever possible with the V200, as the amount of miles logged on this locomotive could easily push it over the edge in the breakdown category.

THE CLASS E III (1977)

DESCRIPTION: This is a refurbishment of the Class E110 and was used extensively for passenger service. More attractive and with a number of improvements, the Class E 111 met the growing demand for passenger service in Germany. Some were modified to be used for S-Bahn service (tramways).

USAGE: Good speed and better reliability edge out other similar choices like the E60 CP.

THE TBX-1 MAGLEV (2008)

DESCRIPTION

A prototype of unparalleled excellence, the TBX-1 utilizes a modified version of the Inductrack design pioneered at the Lawrence Livermore National Laboratory (LLNL). This Bergantz Transport Maglev Prototype glides over retrofitted rail using standard overhead electric caternaries for its initial power, resting on standard trucks until magnetic transition occurs. Once a speed of 2 mph is attained, the Halbach Arrays—in conjunction with submerged passive coil systems—levitate the engine and its refitted cargo, and smoothly propel them to speeds in excess of 280 mph.

USAGE:

If you can afford it, buy one—it's simply too cool and nothing else moves this fast. Is it economical? Probably not, but just one can serve an entire country, provided it doesn't have the size of the United States.

5

Building Your Railroad Empire

BEYOND BASIC STRATEGIES AND TIPS, THERE ARE MANY THINGS YOU NEED TO BECOME EXPERT AT BUILDING AN IRON EMPIRE THAT WILL STAND THE TEST OF TIME. THIS SECTION WILL GIVE YOU DETAILED INSIGHT INTO THOSE AREAS AND SHOULD GET YOU ON THE RIGHT TRACK IN NO TIME.

STATIONS

Stations are second in importance only to your trains. Without them, you cannot pick up or drop off your cargo. However, their function does not stop there. Stations also allow you to maintain your trains, increase revenue, and increase the productivity of the industries you service. They connect you to the rest of the world, so the more strategically you place and improve them, the more efficient that link is.

DIFFERENT TYPES AND FLAVORS

Stations come in three different sizes (Small, Medium, and Large) and five different architectural styles (Victorian, Colonial, Mission Revival, Tudor, and Kyoto Revival). The different architectural styles are purely cosmetic, and do not affect the gameplay. The game will automatically select an architectural style for certain maps, territories, and cities when the architectural style selection is on Default (first selection to the upper right of the station size pictures). However, if you prefer one particular style, or wish to be able to know on sight that a station is yours, you can choose one of the other styles. Your selection will remain the same until you exit the program.

SIZE DOES MATTER

Understanding the difference in the three sizes is critical to your game. Small stations only cost $50,000 and cover an area of 5 squares by 5 squares on the map. Medium stations cost $100,000, but cover a circle with a 9-square diameter for a total of 2.9 times the area. Large stations come in at a $200,000 price tag, and cover a circle with a 17-square diameter. This amounts to 3.5 times the medium station's usable collection area and an incredible 10.2 times that of the small station!

This doesn't always mean that the large station is desirable. If that additional area isn't being used, the extra cash you paid is simply gone. Whether you place a station in an area and which size you use should be determined by two factors: how much room is available, and how many resources you can cover.

Construction space usually only comes into play in the crowded cities. There should be more than enough room to place a large station and connecting track in any city, though rivers and coastline can make for a tight fit. However, if a competitor has already placed a station in the area, you may be forced to squeeze in a small station or none at all. On the flip side, this also means that if you monopolize the space in the middle of the city with your own station and track before another player (computer or human) can place a station, you can force your competition to look elsewhere for revenue!

Resource coverage can be a trickier issue. Generally, it makes more sense to place a large station in the large cities and a small station in the outlying countryside. But this is not always the case. If you only plan on using the steel mill from a large city, there is no need for a large or medium station. Industries such as steel mills, canneries, and oil refineries produce more cargo as you supply them with other materials. The situation changes when you are using many other industries. Mines produce at a set rate that never changes. Farm production can be enhanced to a certain extent by supplying fertilizer or grain, but still reach a limit and cannot produce any more per year. As a result, a single grain farm or coal mine rarely produces enough cargo to make the run profitable. Because of this, you will often find it better to build a medium or large station that is able to cover multiple industries. Two or three grain farms, or a combination of a wool farm and a produce orchard, can easily produce enough to keep your route profitable and your cars full.

Your goodwill and industry profit are both determined in part by how well you service your industries. If you place a large station to cover five cotton farms, you may find your station producing more cotton than you can ship away. None of the cotton farms will be serviced enough to make money, and the extra freight at the station will drop your goodwill. And if you are not careful in setting up the routes, you can end up with more trains than even double track can support. Your railway will become congested in the area, and profit will drop. If you find this happening, try to extend track in opposite directions from your station and haul an even amount in both directions to different textile mills, steel mills, and so on.

As a general rule of thumb, small stations will cover a village—the smallest of settlements. Medium stations can cover towns and small cities, and large stations can cover the most sprawling megalopolises. A cleverly placed large station can sometimes also cover two small villages or towns, increasing the number of houses high enough to create a demand for food and goods that would not be demanded by a single village otherwise. Outside of settlements, size will depend on how many industries you want to draw from.

OTHER PLACEMENT CONSIDERATIONS

There is more to placing a station than coverage. If you are placing a station before running track to the site, pick one of the eight orientation choices to make the station line up with the direction the track will be coming from. Trains that pull straight into a station and can leave straight out again will have a faster turnaround time than one that hits a turn right before and after.

The area the station draws from is determined by the track in front of the station, not the station itself. It doesn't matter which side of the tracks the station is on does not affect area, nor does the orientation of the station.

When two stations co-inhabit a single city, or otherwise share the same industry, the resources produced appear in both stations on a first-come-first-serve manner. Whichever train arrives at and leaves a station first gets the cargo produced. This means that you will be sharing the cargo with your competitor. Even if you do a better job of servicing the station and win the lion's share of the freight, it will not be as high as the amount you would otherwise be able to ship. This means that a station that services more than one industry can still be unprofitable, so choose to share space carefully. It can be a great way to steal revenue from your competition, but you will need to make sure you don't cripple yourself in the attempt.

STATIONS FROM THE INSIDE

You will need to buy improvements for the stations you build. Improvements can decide the success or failure of your route. The list of station upgrades available for purchase fall into one of five types. Not all buildings are desirable or useful at all stations. You should also know when to buy which upgrade. The upgrades also become available in different years and for a range of prices. (For more details on station improvements see Table 5-1.)

TABLE 5-1. STATION IMPROVEMENTS

TYPE	UPGRADE	YEAR	COST	DESCRIPTION
Station Size	Station, Medium	1830*	$100,000	Upgrade to Medium Station
Station Size Station	Station, Large	1830	$200,000	Upgrade to Large
Reduction to Turnaround Time delays by 50%	Customs House	1830	$25,000	Reduce customs
Reduction to Turnaround Time turnaround by 25%	Telegraph Poles	1837	$40,000	Reduce station
Reduction to Turnaround Time	Telephone Poles	1905	$80,000	Reduce station turnaround by 50%
Increase to Passenger Revenue	Saloon	1830	$16,000	10% increase to passenger revenue
Increase to Passenger Revenue	Restaurant, Small	1830	$50,000	20% increase to passenger revenue
Increase to Passenger Revenue	Restaurant, Large	1850	$100,000	30% increase to passenger revenue
Increase to Passenger Revenue	Hotel, Small	1830	$65,000	20% increase to passenger revenue
Increase to Passenger Revenue	Hotel, Large	1878	$175,000	40% increase to passenger revenue
Reduction to Pickup Delay Penalty	Warehouse	1830	$25,000	50% reduction in pickup delay penalty for goods, cotton and wool
Reduction to Pickup Delay Penalty	Post Office	1840	$35,000	50% reduction in pickup delay penalty for mail
Reduction to Pickup Delay Penalty	Refrigerated Storage	1860	$50,000	50% reduction in pickup delay penalty for roduce and milk.
Reduction to Pickup Delay Penalty	Grain Silo	1873	$35,000	50% reduction in pickup delay penalty for grain, coffee, and sugar.
Reduction to Pickup Delay Penalty	Liquid Storage	1885	$50,000	50% reduction in pickup delay penalty for oil and chemicals.
Train Performance	Water Tower	1830	$25,000	Refills water in steam engines. Steam engines without water travel much slower.

Type	Upgrade	Year	Cost	Description
Train Performance	Sanding Tower	1830	$30,000	Refills sand. Trains without sand travel 50% slower
Train Performance	Roundhouse	1830	$120,000	Provides maintenance (oil). Low oil increasesrisk of breakdown/crash

1830 means upgrade is available at beginning of all games

The first type of upgrade is simply a larger station. If you have purchased a small or medium station, the larger station size(s) will appear on the purchase list, allowing you to upgrade to a station that draws from a larger area. The cost to do so is the same as the original structure would have been, so it is not an efficient way to build a large station. However, a lot of times when you are low on cash, it is a good idea to place a smaller station in a location and start a route, then upgrade when you can afford to do so.

The second type of upgrade available is the type that decreases turnaround time. Decreasing turnaround time gets your train back on its route quicker, to pick up more cargo for more cash, which means more money for you. There are three upgrades that improve turnaround time:

- **Telegraph Poles** are available in 1837 for $40,000, and they decrease the base turnaround time by 25 percent.

- **Telephone Poles** become available in 1905, with a price tag of $80,000. They replace Telegraph Poles, reducing the base turnaround by 50 percent.

- **Customs Houses** reduce *customs* delays by 50 percent. This means that they only have an effect when a train ships cargo into another territory or to a port. Customs delays can be quite lengthy without a Customs House.

The third type of upgrade includes buildings that increase the revenue you receive from passengers:

- **Small Restaurant**—1830, $50,000, 20 percent increase in revenue. This is the first restaurant you can build.

- **Large Restaurant**—late 1850, $100,000, 30 percent increase in revenue. You can add one of these instead of, or as an upgrade to an existing restaurant.

- **Saloon**—1830, $16,000, 10 percent increase in revenue. The Saloon doesn't give a huge increase in passenger revenues, but coupled with a Small Restaurant, it's worth adding.

- **Small Hotel**—1830, $65,000, 20 percent increase in revenue. Passengers like being able to stay near their departure point. Use this structure to get a solid boost to revenue.

- **Large Hotel**—late 1878, $175, 40 percent increase in revenue With double the revenue increase of a Small Hotel, the Large Hotel should be added as soon as it becomes available.

The Large Restaurants and hotels replace their diminutive counterparts. These upgrades only affect passenger revenue, but on many maps, that revenue is no laughing matter. Only add these upgrades to stations that you plan on using as passenger stops; they have no purpose at cargo stops. But at a potential increase of 80 percent to the most lucrative industry in the game, these five buildings can be used to create significant income.

> THE INDUSTRIES CAN SURVIVE WITHOUT YOUR RAIL SERVICE, BUT IF YOU DO A GOOD JOB WITHIN A PARTICULAR AREA, YOU'LL REALLY SEE IT THRIVE, WHICH HAS LOTS OF NICE SIDE EFFECTS FOR YOUR RAILROAD—THE MOST IMPORTANT OF WHICH IS THAT MORE CARGOES ARE AVAILABLE TO HAUL.

The fourth upgrade category holds those structures that reduce the penalty for delays in freight pickup. This does not mean that the revenue you receive is affected at all. Instead, the amount available to deliver is increased. When cargo is ready for pickup, it slowly degrades. Overtime, that cargo will dwindle and be lost. These upgrades reduce the rate at which this happens for resources that would otherwise quickly decay and should be placed in the station that is *collecting* the materials:

- **Post Offices** (late 1840, $35,000) keep citizens happy and mail organized, reducing the penalty for delays in *mail* pickup by 50 percent.

- **Refrigerated Storage units** (late 1860, $50,000) prevent spoilage in *produce* and *milk*, reducing their delay penalties by 50 percent.

- **Warehouses** (1830, $25,000) protect *goods*, *cotton*, and *wool* from the environment, also for a 50 percent reduction in delay penalties.

- **Liquid Storage units** (late 1885, $50,000) protect *oil* and *chemicals* from the environment and offer a 50 percent reduction in delay penalties.

- **Grain Silos** (late 1873, $35,000) reduce the penalties for *grain*, *coffee*, and *sugar* by 50 percent. Other resources such as coal and iron do not degrade nearly as quickly, so they do not have special structures for storage.

The final type of upgrade, and perhaps the most important one, is used to maintain the performance of your engines. Without these upgrades, your engines will at best slow to a crawl and at worst simply crash on the tracks, resulting in the loss of an expensive engine and all the cargo it was hauling, as well as in the delay of all trains following closely behind it. While the other station improvements are optional, these three are vitally important. Do not let a train operate for too long without the benefit of these upgrades, all of which are available at the start of the game:

- **Sanding Towers**—All trains use sand from Sanding Towers ($30,000) for traction. Without sand, trains will run twice as slow. They will use sand much more slowly on flat ground, but can use up their supply very quickly when they hit steep grades, slowing them down even more. Since some of the resources such as grain, wool, milk, food and others are time-sensitive, the reduction in speed not only increases delivery time but also reduces the amount you receive when you do deliver the cargo.

- **Water Towers**—Only steam engines use water from Water Towers ($25,000), so they are not required if you are only running diesel or electric engines. However, the reduction in speed from a lack of water is even greater than the already considerable reduction from a lack of sand. Steam engines without water will creep along at only a small fraction of their potential.

- **Roundhouses**—All three engine types require maintenance from Roundhouses ($120,000). Roundhouses keep oil levels full, so if an engine travels too far without maintenance, its chance of breakdown or crashing significantly rises.

> TRAINS DO NOT NEED TO STOP AT A STATION IN ORDER TO REFILL THEIR SAND, WATER, AND OIL. THEY ONLY NEED TO PASS THROUGH. SMALL STATIONS ARE, IN ESSENCE, ONLY DEPOTS. TREAT THEM AS SUCH. DO NOT BE AFRAID TO PLACE SMALL STATIONS ALONG LONG ROUTES AS "REFILLING DEPOTS." GIVE THEM A SANDING TOWER, A WATER TOWER, AND, IF NEEDED, A ROUNDHOUSE. NOTHING ELSE. THIS WILL PROVIDE A CHEAP AND EASY WAY TO KEEP YOUR TRAINS RUNNING SMOOTH AND FAST.

When you are using steam engines, it is a good idea to have a Water Tower at every station. Sanding Towers can be put at every other one if distances are not too great, but as soon as a route goes into the mountains, Sanding Towers at every station are not a bad idea. Roundhouses do not need to be as common, which is a good thing considering their cost. Place them at central hubs that a lot of trains pass through. Make sure every train goes through a station that has a Roundhouse, though. And while there is no negative impact from low sand or water—only running completely out of sand or water— this is not the case for maintenance. The lower a train is on oil, the more expensive its maintenance and the higher the chance that it will break down or crash. So while they are not needed at every station, more is always better.

The key to placing Roundhouses, Sanding Towers, and Water Towers effectively is to watch your trains and figure out what spots they travel past the most. This can be a particular station, or a crossroads on the map. A crossroads can provide a perfect opportunity for a refilling depot to service your trains. Place refilling depots along particularly long stretches of track to refill sand and water, and place one in mountainous areas with a Sanding Tower to refill sand as needed. Trains will use their sand quickly in the mountains, so be sure to watch them and place a depot as often as is required. One good idea is to provide a Sanding Tower on each side of a large ridge, or in valleys between multiple ridges.

MANAGING YOUR STATIONS

Okay, now you know where to put your stations most effectively, and you know how to wisely decide on your upgrades. However, the next thing you know, you'll have 30 or 40 stations and you won't be able to keep them all straightened out. You need a lesson in station management.

FINDING STATION INFORMATION

There are five locations for station information and management, but they are just different ways of getting to and looking at the same data—which ones you use is your decision.

Main Window

The first is in the *Main Window* itself. When you hold your general cursor over a station—one of yours or a competitor's—the area it collects from will "light up." Right-click and hold on the station, and a floating window will appear that displays supply, demand, and the To and From coins.

World Overview

The second way to learn about your stations (and all other players' stations) is to use the *World Overview: Stations*. Click the World Overview button on the left of the screen and select

View Station Statuses (second from the top on the right side of the Center List Box), or use this option's hotkey 7 (not on the number pad) at any time. Suddenly every station will be connected by a green line to a small box displaying supply as text only and the To and From coins. These boxes will remain until you select another action, or exit the Worldview mode.

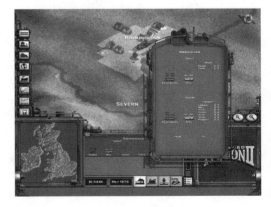

Center List Box

The next location is in the *Center List Box* itself, inside the main world. Clicking on the Station Tab below it will change the Center List Box to display station information for stations that you own. This will show the information for two stations at a time, with supply and the To and From coins, but not demand. To view more stations at once, click the small up-arrow button above the list. This will expand the list to show seven station boxes at once. The slider bar to the right scrolls up and down the list. Clicking on the list shows an action view of the station in the video window to the right, and clicking on that window will center the Main Window on that station. Right-clicking on one of the boxes in the List Box will also bring up the box you saw when you right-clicked the station itself in the Main Window.

Station Detail Screen

More information is shown in the *Station Detail Screen.* This screen can be reached in several ways: a) by double-clicking the station in the main window; b) by double-clicking the station's box in the Center List Box; c) by double-clicking the station's box in the Station List Screen (we'll get to that in a moment); d) by clicking the Single Item Detail button at

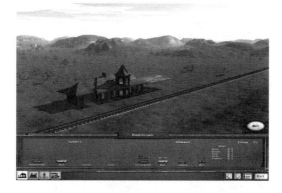

the bottom right of the Station List Screen; and e) by clicking the Station Tab at the bottom of the screen while in Train, Personal, or Company Detail Screens. This is the same place in which you purchase upgrades. This is also the only location in the game that shows which upgrades are in your station. The top portion shows the station and all of its upgrades. Moving the cursor over a structure in this view will display the structure's name along the bottom of the screen. Below the station shot is an area that shows the station's full supply and demand needs and the To and From coins. The arrow buttons at the bottom of the screen scroll through the stations in the order in which they were built.

Station List Screen

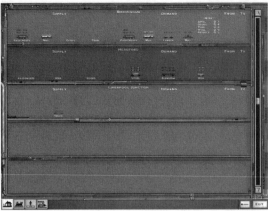

The final location for station info, and one of the most useful, is the Station List Screen. This screen can be reached by clicking the bulleted List Screen button at the bottom right side of the Center List Box of the Station Detail Screen. This list screen shows five stations at a time, but in much more detail than the Center List Boxes.

INTERPRETING STATION INFORMATION

Now that you know how to navigate through all of the station screens, here's what all the details mean:

Supply

Supply tells you what the station makes. A zero by the word or no freight icons above it means that there is currently none of that cargo at the station. This could either be because all of the produced resource has been hauled away or because the station needs to be provided with other resources in order to make the new material.

Demand

Demand shows what the station wants to receive. If there is a number beside the demand, or freight icons above it, this tells you how high of a demand the station has for it: "9" is the highest level of demand, and "0" is the lowest. A demand of "0" means that the station has all it needs for the moment but, if not supplied, will increase demand again later. Try to keep a station's demand above "0." When playing the Expert financial model, keep the demand as high as possible—higher demand will result in higher revenue in return (see Table 5-2).

TABLE 5-2. REVENUE MODIFIER FOR THE EXPERT FINANCIAL MODEL

STATION DEMAND	REVENUE MODIFIER
0	50%
1	60%
2	70%
3	80%
4	90%
5	100%
6	110%
7	120%
8	130%
9	140%

As Table 5-2 shows, you lose half your money by supplying a station with a cargo that is at "0" demand, while you receive extra revenue above the average freight price for supplying to a station with a demand at "9."

To and From Coins

The To and From coins represent how much money that station has made. The coins refresh each year. To shows how much money has been made from freight brought into the station, and From shows how much money has been made from freight hauled away to another station. This means that every coin in the To list of one station is also shown on the From list of another station, and vice-versa.

A quick glance of the To and From coins will show you which stations are most profitable, and whether that is from resources supplied or demanded. Using the Center List Box lists (expanded or not) is perfect for showing you the supply waiting to be picked up. Periodically run down the list and look for large surplus. This will tell you what stations need to be serviced better. Remember, keeping a low surplus improves your goodwill, which in some campaigns is vital to success. The Station List is perfect for showing supply and demand. It's easy to find stations that have surplus—potential revenue—and high demand, or deficit, so you know what stations are the most profitable places to take your surplus. High demand can also indicate great opportunities for expansion.

TRACK MECHANICS

Before you can run trains, you'll need to lay down track on which they can run. This will start off as only a short run or two, but by the end of the game will often become a vast, expansive web of interconnected (and separate) routes. And there is a lot more to the process than simply stretching out lengths of rails and ties.

The manner in which track is laid in *Railroad Tycoon II* is different than in the original *Railroad Tycoon*. Instead of using the keyboard, track is now laid by clicking the beginning point (or, if you wish, anywhere in the middle) and holding the mouse button while moving the mouse. A length of track will snake its way from the beginning point to your cursor, in the shortest path possible. This is not, however, usually the cheapest or best route. The shortest route for the track is not always the fastest path for a train. More on laying track effectively will be covered in the section, "Routes: Setting Them up and Making Them Work." Upgrading track is done by dragging new track over the old. Bulldozing is neither required nor recommended, since it will make the upgrade much more expensive.

TRACK TYPES

Track comes in several different types. Of course, there is plain Single Track, but there is also Double Track, Single Electrified Track, and Double Electrified Track. On top of that, there are three types of bridges that can be selected, for use with any type of track.

- **Single Track**—Trains on Single Track can only occupy space one train at a time. If one train is already in an area on the track, any other train will stop until the first train has moved on. Which train has right of way at such a meeting depends mainly on its Priority setting. Lower priority trains always stop for higher priority trains. If two trains of the same priority meet, whichever train entered the grid square first wins right of way. However, all competitors' trains on your track automatically have lower priority than any of yours, and any train you send onto track owned by another company receives lower priority than a train owned by that same company.

- **Double Track**—Double track lays two separate lines down. Trains always stay to the right side of the track, relative to which direction they are traveling. This creates a cycle, with all traffic going one direction staying on the same side. This means that no trains will meet head to head with another. Trains can and will still overtake other trains from behind, forcing one of them to stop and yield right of way. However, despite this, the efficiency gained by upgrading to double track can be much higher than a factor of two. If a particular length of track is only being used by one train, there is no improvement in run time. Two trains can sometimes run on a single track without too much congestion. Three or more trains are almost always too much for a single stretch of track. The general rule is that if a train spends more than ten percent of its time between stations yielded to other trains, it is losing too much revenue.

- **Electric Track**—Electric trains cannot run without electrified track. Without it, electrified trains will sit at the station with a notice reading, "No Electricity." A lightning bolt behind a red circle with a diagonal red line across it will also appear to the right of that. As soon as the track is upgraded to electrified track, the notice and symbol will disappear and the train will begin its run. Both steam and diesel engines run on electric track normally.

There are three types of bridges: wooden, stone, and steel. Table 5-3 lists the costs, year they become available, and special restrictions of these bridges.

TABLE 5-3. BRIDGE TYPES

| TYPE | YEAR AVAILABLE | COST (ON FLAT GROUND) | | SPECIAL RESTRICTIONS |
		SINGLE TRACK	DOUBLE TRACK	
Wooden	1830	$60,000	n.a.	Only available in single track; trains slow down 40 percent while crossing
Stone	1840	$200,000	$300,000	None
Steel	1880	$150,000	$225,000	Trains slow down 20 percent while crossing

Note that trains slow down on the wooden and steel bridges, and that wooden bridges can only be built as single track. The bridge costs are the same for electric track, but the bridge itself must be upgraded (at no cost) when track is upgraded from normal to electric before an electric train can run on it.

LAYING TRACK

When track is being built, numbers float above each segment of track. The white numbers indicate cost, while the green, yellow, and red numbers represent the grade for that square. Green grade is good, ranging from 0 to 1.9 percent grade. Yellow numbers indicate grades from 2 percent to 3.9 percent. Red numbers, 4 percent grade and higher, represent steep grades that should be avoided when possible.

For quick reference, Table 5-4 shows the *base* track costs.

TABLE 5-4: BASE TRACK COSTS

BASE TRACK COSTS (PER SQUARE)	NON-ELECTRIFIED	ELECTRIFIED
Single	$4,000	$10,000
Double	$6,000	$15,000

However, your track cost will rarely fit this table. There are a number of factors that will affect the cost of track building:

- **Grades**—Low grades do not significantly change the cost of track, but steeper grades can result in significantly higher cost for those squares.

- **Terrain**—Track building on sand (beach and desert terrain) costs 25 percent more. Swampy and mountainous terrain add 50 percent to the cost, and building on snow doubles it. In addition, every tree that needs to be cut down in order to lay track adds an extra $1,000. This is an insignificant amount in the plains and slightly woodsy areas, but the cost can jump significantly in forested areas. In fact, in the most heavily forested areas the expense can almost become prohibitive.

- **Terraforming**—When track is built, the ground is made flat perpendicular to the direction the rails run. This will add little to the majority of your track laying. However, it can become very expensive when you build your track along the side of a mountain or along a steep coastline. You can often find low grades this way; however, you will pay a lot of money for the luxury.

- **Upgrading**—The cost of upgrades changes depending on the type of both the old and new track. The only time you do not save money in upgrading is when you improve single track to double electrified track. In this case, the cost of laying the double electrified track starts at a base of $15, the same as new double electrified track. Downgrading is not allowed, and upgrading double track to electrified *single* costs the same as double track to electrified *double* (and it creates the same result—electrified double).

Track can only intersect at 45- and 135-degree angles, not at 90 degrees. When one track is dragged to connect to another track at 90 degrees, the computer will automatically turn the track at an angle before it connects in order to make a viable intersection. If one track is dragged across another so that a right angle is made, trains will not be able to turn at that intersection and it will not count as "connecting track." As a final note, track cannot be laid across ocean or through an existing building.

ROUTES: SETTING THEM UP AND MAKING THEM WORK

Of course, infrastructure involves more than just knowing how to put track where you want it. You also need to know where you need to put it! In other words, you need to become proficient at route planning.

GENERAL TIPS

Most important is learning to work with the drag-laying technique. The computer calculates the shortest route, but this is often not the best. It is fine when you are laying track across flat ground, but can create steep grades when you get into the hills. A better method is to drag short sections at a time, creating long runs section by section. You can often avoid steep grades by zooming in and dragging track around hills and mountains, or along the faces of slopes, as opposed to straight over or across them. Some very intimidating landscapes can actually be managed without ever getting above a 3% grade this way. The resulting track may be longer and slightly more expensive, but your trains will be able to travel from station to station much more quickly.

IN SCENARIOS WHERE YOU MUST KEEP YOUR ENTIRE TRACK CONNECTED, YOU CAN STILL REACH THOSE OUT-OF-THE-WAY CITIES, SUCH AS CITIES ALONG A MOUNTAINOUS COAST OPPOSITE FROM YOUR STARTING POINT. SIMPLY BUILD A CONNECTING TRACK OVER THE MOUNTAINS—DISREGARDING THE GRADE FOR THE MOMENT—AND THEN CONNECT THE TWO CITIES TO THIS LINE. NOW, BULLDOZE THAT NASTY, STEEP GRADE CONNECTING TRACK, AND YOU HAVE EXPANDED TO TWO "UNREACHABLE" CITIES.

Steep grades are not always to be feared, though. If a coal mine is at the top of a mountain, you can bet that you won't ever need to haul anything up to the coal mine. Most trains, especially the ones that perform well on grades, can run up a mountain at a decent speed as long as it is not hauling any freight cars behind it. Run the engine up by itself, and the engine and loaded coal cars will shoot down the grade at close to top speed.

KEEP AN EYE OUT FOR CITIES AND INDUSTRIES AT THE EDGE OF A STEEP CLIFF. YOU CAN OFTEN PLACE A STATION AT THE BASE OR TOP OF THAT CLIFF AND STILL DRAW FROM THE INDUSTRIES AND HOUSES ON THE OTHER SIDE OF THE STEEP GRADE, WITHOUT EVER NEEDING A HIGH GRADE PERFORMING ENGINE!

Trains slow down at turns, so try to keep your track as straight as the land allows. Trains slowing down at a turn can cause others behind it to stop, cutting into your revenues and reducing the efficiency of your lines. The distance you wish to span will depend on the trains you use and cargoes you haul. In general, later years will make longer routes desirable.

> ONE TRICK TO OVERCOMING STEEP GRADES IS TO DELIBERATELY TERRAFORM THE GROUND. HOWEVER, THIS CAN BE AN EXTREMELY EXPENSIVE PROSPECT. THE BENEFIT IS REDUCTION OF A TERRIBLE SLOPE (10 PERCENT GRADES AND MORE) TO AROUND 1 PERCENT OR 2 PERCENT. DRAG A LENGTH OR TWO OF TRACK AT THE BEGINNING OF THE STEEP GRADES, PERPENDICULAR TO THE DIRECTION YOU WANT FOR YOUR FINAL TRACK, AND WITH THE FIRST SQUARE OF THE TRACK AT THE LEVEL YOU WANT THE GROUND TO BE AT. THE LAND WILL BE RAISED OR LOWERED TO THIS NEW LEVEL. A ROW OF THESE SHORT TRACKS WILL CREATE A FLAT AREA. BULLDOZE THESE MICRO-TRACKS, AND LAY THE "REAL" TRACK ROUTE. AT A HEFTY PRICE, YOU CAN MOVE MOUNTAINS!

Track costs money to maintain. If you are planning to expand, save up until you have enough money to lay your track, place your station, and start a train. This will keep you from paying track maintenance costs for track that isn't "earning its keep."

TRACK SYSTEMS

There are several different overall systems to use when laying track. All of them are useful, but you should choose the one that best fits your current application.

MAIN LINE

A main line system is when your railway has one long line connecting two distant cities. Main lines connect the two cities by making a wavy line across the landscape, jumping from one smaller city to another. A combination of different routes can be set up, leapfrogging passengers from one city to another that is two cities away. Passengers from the city in between these two can then be sent to another farther away. This will allow you to haul all of your passengers, while increasing the distance to gain greater revenue. Send a few more trains from one end of the main line to the other, and you will make a lot of money when the trains finally pull in. These routes could take years to finish, but are usually very lucrative.

Most players will quickly realize that too many trains will congest a main line. Other players will not be able to pass up industry deposits close by. This is when using a Spur system becomes a good idea.

SPUR SYSTEM

Spurs are small tracks that shoot off from the main line to hit a station or two. These spurs can be single lines, or small loops that reconnect farther down the line so that trains can rejoin the main line without doubling back. These loops, or pockets, not only shorten a train's travelling distance to the next station, but also help fight congestion.

LOOP OR CIRCUIT

A different system that is very efficient is the Loop or Circuit. Not necessarily round, this system allows a train to start at one end of an industry flow and carry that all the way to the end product. For example, a train can pick up grain from a grain farm and haul it to a sheep farm, where it picks up a load of wool and carries it to a textile mill. There it converts the wool into goods and hauls them to a large city that is close to the initial grain farm. This system makes money at every step along the way, and creates its own product as it goes. The drawback to trying to use this system is that the opportunity to run a track that utilizes every step of the industry flow and ends up near the first step rarely presents itself.

HUB

Another good system is the Hub system. In this system, one large city serves as a central hub, and smaller routes and spurs eventually create lucrative supplies for this central city. This is a good system because large cities have high demands. The problem is that even the largest of cities can only take so much, and some industries such as auto production often only pop up in larger cities. Your hub city will grow and produce its own cars and passengers, but you will not have any good location to take them to. You also find your hub city quickly becoming congested as many of your trains fight to deliver cargo to one or two central stations.

WEB

The Hub system's shortcoming naturally leads to the extensive Web system. This system connects several hubs into a large web network. You feed your large cities in routes just like in the Hub system, but you can then exchange goods between the large cities, as well. Since your trains are dispersed across the web, congestion is kept down and demand is kept up.

BROKEN LINE

The final system is the Broken Line system. This is simply making small routes wherever you find a lucrative one. You may have a couple stations connected by track hauling passengers on the east side of the map, another on the west side creating goods and shipping them to a port, and another in the north making steel.

In practice, players will automatically use a combination of these systems, shaped by the industry distribution, goals, and politics of each map. Some maps do not allow the Broken Line system, only permitting players to build from existing track. For example, the Orient Express scenario lends itself to a combination of a hub or web in France (between Paris and Orleans) with a main line extending far across the continent to Constantinople. This line, then, may have spurs extending from it. Other times, a main line might have spurs that become other main lines.

What system you use will affect how you upgrade your stations. Depending on how far apart your cities are, you might wish to put a Water Tower in every station, a Sanding Tower in every other, and a Roundhouse in every third. In a Hub or Web system, the central cities are perfect locations for your Roundhouses. Sanding Towers and Water Towers will be placed in outlying stations, as distance requires. When using spurs, use the cities on the main line to which the spurs attach as your roundhouse stations. This will supply oil to both the engines on your spurs and the ones passing through that main line city. If the spurs are not too long, you may not have to place a Sanding or Water Tower in them, either.

PLAYING WITH THE AI— WHAT TO EXPECT

AI PLAYERS' STRATEGIES WILL BE DIFFERENT IN GENERAL, BUT THERE ARE SOME BASIC GUIDELINES TO REMEMBER:

- AI PLAYERS WILL EXPAND IN OPEN, FLAT AREAS AND SHY AWAY FROM MOUNTAINOUS AREAS.
- WHEN THEY DO LAY TRACK IN THE MOUNTAINS, THEY WILL OFTEN LAY TRACK WITH VERY STEEP GRADES.
- AI PLAYERS MAKE MOST OF THEIR MONEY FROM PASSENGERS AND MAIL, LEAVING INDUSTRY ROUTES MOSTLY OPEN FOR YOU TO CAPITALIZE FROM.
- THIS ALSO PROVIDES ONE OF THEIR WEAKNESSES, SINCE YOU KNOW WHAT CARGO THEY DEPEND ON (PASSENGERS AND MAIL), YOU KNOW WHAT TO STEAL. YOU CAN MAKE UP THE MONEY WITH INDUSTRIES, BUT THE AI WILL ONLY TRY TO FIND MORE PASSENGERS.
- THE AI RARELY BUILDS ALL OF THE UPGRADES IT COULD BENEFIT FROM IN ITS STATIONS. IF YOU MERGE WITH AN AI-CONTROLLED COMPANY, BE SURE TO CHECK AND UPGRADE YOUR NEW STATIONS.

MANAGING YOUR COMPANY

With the fundamentals of infrastructure management under your belt, it's time to discuss the other important aspects of the game—managing your company, and managing yourself. This section covers company management, focusing on using the Company Detail Screen to best advantage.

The Company Detail Screen contains everything you need to understand the financial state of your company. However, there are plenty of details here, and the book can be intimidating at first. This section helps you understand your company, as well as your competition, section by section, and page by page.

OVERVIEW

The Overview section gives an overall view of the company: Name, Logo, Year Established, Chairman, Manager, Total Debt and Revenue to Date—it's all in this section. Most of these items are self-explanatory:

- **Company Logo**—The picture at the top of this and every page is your company's logo. You'll see it again in the Stock Market portfolio, in the Company List Boxes, and floating over your properties in the Main Window.

- **Portrait**—The portrait at the top of the first page is you. As the caption beside the picture states, you are the Chairman of your company. Below that is your game persona. In single-player games, you become a historical figure, while in multiplayer you are able to give yourself any name you choose. Immediately beneath your name are your current salary and a statement on how happy (or unhappy) your investors are. Both are affected by how you run your company. For more information on your character, right-click and hold on your picture or description. Your description and a brief statement of personal wealth will appear in a window.

- **Manager**—Below your personal information is a picture and description of your current manager: his name, salary, and what bonuses or penalties you receive from him. For a more detailed description on him as a person (often explaining his bonuses as well), right-click his picture or description.

At the bottom of the page are the options to hire another manager or resign from your position as chairman. You may do the former many times in a game, but you'll rarely do the latter unless it makes sense for you to take over a company where you own a majority of the shares. If you are playing in expert financial mode and own more than 10 percent of a company's stock, that company's book will show an option that reads, "Call for Special Chairman election." If you opt to do this, all shareholders vote on the matter. If you succeed (either because of a majority if investors think you are a better chairman or because you own more than 50 percent of the stock), you become the new chairman. This is *not* a merger. Your previous company becomes controlled by a committee until another player, either human or computer, assumes chairmanship of it. This is a great way to "abandon ship" of a sinking company. Since only companies can merge, the special election is also a great way for a player to gain control of a new company if he has been fired.

The facing page begins with your company's name and the year in which it was established, followed by the current year's revenue to date (money made directly from industries and cargo) and profit to date (total revenue and interest minus expenses, or net income).

Following that are cash (currently available for spending) and debt (bonds outstanding). The pair of figures below that shows the current total length of track mileage your company controls and the average speed of your trains. After that is your goodwill standing, which can range from atrocious to perfect. Goodwill will be covered more extensively in the Territories section.

Finishing the second page of the Overview section are two options, Change Company Name/Logo, and Next. Change Company Name/Logo can be used to give your company a fresh look and sound any time you like, but in no way affects its finances. Next takes you to the next page in the Overview.

On the left side of the next page is an Efficiency Statement for the current year. Starting off this list are Loads Hauled (the total number of freight and passenger cars delivered to date in the current year) and Load Miles Hauled. Load Miles Hauled refers to how many miles freight has been transported. It is a measure of how many loads of cargo have passed over the average mile of track. If you haul four loads of cargo over your track in one year, your Load Miles Hauled will be four times the total length of your track. Listed next are Haulage Revenues (total revenue from cargo deliveries only) and Revenues Per Load Mile (the average profit made per each mile each load of cargo traveled—higher denotes better efficiency). Next are Fuel Costs (for the year to date) and Fuel Costs Per Load Mile (fuel costs divided by Load Mile Hauled—this time, the lower number is better). The next pair of figures lists Track Miles (same as on prior page) and Load Miles Per Track Miles. This number tells you how many loads you are managing to haul over the average mile of track. A higher number is better, meaning that you are making efficient use of the track you have.

The final figure on this page lists the Average Speed (of your trains).

One important note on efficiency is that what is "good" will change over time. Cargo load prices will change, new trains will use more fuel per mile, trains will travel faster, you will need fewer trains to haul your cargo, and the market will change from Boom Times to Depression and back again. The best measure of efficiency is to compare your figures to other companies during the same time period, taking differences in route, trains, and cargo into account.

The remaining pages in Overview are total Efficiency pages for prior years, so that you can see how your efficiency rating changes over time.

MEN, MACHINES, AND INDUSTRIES

Income

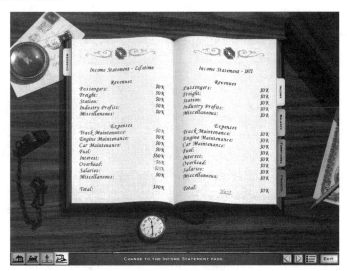

The Income section itemizes your revenues and expenses. The first page in the section gives your Lifetime figures. Revenues and expenses are separated, with Revenues listed first. At the top of its list are Passengers and Freight.

Passengers and Freight

Passengers are by far the most common and important cargo. They are also different from all others. Only passengers have upgrades within the stations devoted solely to increasing revenue from them. People are more sensitive to how quickly they are delivered than any other cargo, and they react more dramatically to being given the opportunity to travel farther distances. They are willing to pay more to ride on a record-setting train.

Your ability to service a city has a direct impact on how many people live there. Other cargo is moved to be used by people, and can create new products. You receive your payment upon delivering the freight. Passengers, however, are moved because they want to be. No new product is created, and the money that you receive at the end of a run is actually representative of the money they paid at the beginning. Houses cannot be purchased as an industry investment, and bulldozing them negatively affects your goodwill standing. In short, passengers are different from all other cargoes, and are treated as such in the Income statement. The Freight line lists revenue from everything else you ship.

Stations

The next item, Station, lists revenue made at the stations. This includes extra revenue from the passenger upgrades. The money your passengers spend at the restaurants, hotels and saloons is found here. This also includes revenue you receive when another company uses your station to deliver goods. Every time another company does so, they pay you a $2,000 station fee per car.

Industry Investments

If you have invested in industries, profit received from them is listed here. This number can be a negative one if some of your industries are losing money. If this is the case, look into either servicing those industries better or selling them. For more on how to service your industries better, please refer to the Economy chapter.

Following Industry revenue, and rounding out the Revenue list, is Miscellaneous. This includes all other revenue, such as payments received for connecting to cities, cash from deals (shady or not) and other random events.

Expenses

Heading the Expenses list are your maintenance costs, split into Track, Engine, and Car maintenance. Just like it sounds, this is the money you spend to keep your track in place, trains running, and freight cars together. They can add up to a fairly hefty amount, but are a necessary evil.

The next figures, Fuel and Engine maintenance, both depend in part on what type of train you use. Some trains use more fuel per load mile hauled and cost more to maintain. However, these costs can be balanced if the train is fast or powerful, thus bringing in more revenue to cover the expense.

Interest is the balance between the amount of interest your company makes from cash in the bank and the interest you pay on bonds outstanding. This number will usually be positive, thus becoming income listed on the Expenses instead of Revenues, but can be negative.

Overhead is a figure that will generally run about 1 percent to 3 percent of your revenue. It represents the assorted costs of running a business—the taxes, fees, licenses, pens, notepads, yellow sticky-notes, coffee, phone bills, and so on.

Following the Overhead figure is Salaries. This is simply the combined total of your salary and that of your manager.

Ending the Expenses list is Miscellaneous. Like the Miscellaneous at the end of the Revenue section, this covers random large expenses encountered throughout the game. Development costs for a new engine, costs for buying rights into a new territory, bribes, er, *fees* paid to "freelance businessmen," and so on.

At the bottom of the page is the Total, or Revenues minus Expenses. You want this number to be positive! You will often have a negative year due to economy cycles, heavy expansion periods and the like. But in general, these need to be kept at a minimum, with other years bringing in heavy revenues.

The facing page contains all of the same figures for the current year to date. The numbers on this page will change as the year advances. By selecting Next at the bottom of this page, you can flip through all of the previous year totals up to the year your company was established.

BALANCE

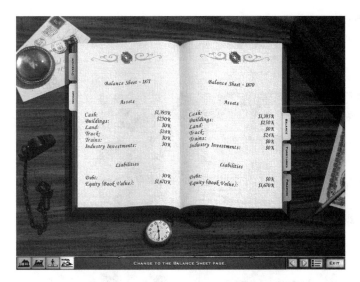

This is on of the most important sections in the book, and should be referenced often. Like the previous sections, it is broken down into the current year-to-date and previous years. This page will show you your Company Net Worth (a.k.a. Equity, a.k.a. Book Value), which is also broken down into your current cash, investments, and physical assets.

Assets and Liabilities

The first item on the list is Cash. This is your current cash available to spend. It is the same figure displayed in the Cash window in the main world view, as well as the figure shown on the second page of the Overview section. Remember, this can be negative, decreasing your total Asset value.

The next few items on the list are your physical assets—buildings, trains, track, and industry investments—all the things you have purchased or paid to build. These count towards your net worth because they have monetary value. This is why your Equity stays positive when your cash or annual income is negative. If you have too many years of negative income, however, you can drive your Equity into the negative range!

Finally, below Liabilities is debt and Equity. Your Equity is calculated by subtracting your debt from your assets. It is the Big Number. It tells you what your company is worth. Keep a sharp eye on this number. In order to keep it high, be sure to expand aggressively, invest heavily in industries, and watch your cash flow.

TERRITORIES

The Territories tab is your link to the political world. It is subdivided into three smaller sections, Political View, Access Rights view, and Goodwill View.

POLITICAL VIEW

The Political View has a view of the current map on the left page. This map shows every territory on the map, each with its own distinct color and pattern. This color pattern matches a swatch on the right side of the page. Beside the swatch are that territory's name, whether you have train-running and track-building rights in that territory, and a Consult button. When the list doesn't fit on one page, you can click Next and Previous to see more of the list. The map will remain on the left side of the page. Train-running rights and track-laying rights can sometimes be purchased separately but are often purchased together. The territories on this list can be countries, states, provinces, or even cities. The nature of the territories will change from map to map.

The Consult button brings up a window that displays your standing with the territory. This window, in essence, sums up a meeting with an ambassador from that territory. It lists your Goodwill Standing with that territory, what access rights you currently possess, and the price that territory will accept in order to grant you any access rights you do not currently possess. Use this view when you want to buy access rights, or when you want to see what your standing is with a particular country.

ACCESS RIGHTS VIEW

Enter the Access Rights View to see a summary of your access rights. The map on the left page will now display your rights within each territory. If you have Full access rights, the territory will be green. Brown territories have given you the right to run track in their land, but not the right to run stations. What this actually means is that you can build infrastructure, including stations, and you may purchase industries.

You cannot run trains on the track, though, and thus cannot service your industries. Yellow denotes the opposite. You can run tracks on existing track, but cannot build any new infrastructure. Finally, red territories have not granted you any rights. You cannot purchase industries, lay track, run trains, or otherwise interact with the territory.

GOODWILL VIEW

Your goodwill standing with each individual territory is shown on the Goodwill View page of the Territories section. The map remains, as in the other two views, but territories will now be filled with a color representing a range from Perfect to Atrocious. The colors fade from Green (Perfect) through yellow to Red (Atrocious). Goodwill is affected mainly by the following factors:

- **Safety and reliability**—Territories will look on you more favorably if you keep your safety and reliability high. Well-maintained trains, the use of cabooses, and good managers can all help you. Conversely, high frequencies of breakdowns, crashes, and robberies can severely damage your political standing.

- **Dependability**—Goodwill is also affected by the dependability of your service. If you haul all the freight provided at a station so that supply is kept low, your goodwill would rise while surpluses at stations will lower your standing.

There are two ways to gain access rights. You can buy them through the Consult option in the Political View, or you can be granted rights through events in the game. Sometimes you will have the ability to purchase either train-running or track-laying rights, but usually the only option is to purchase all rights or none at all.

When you begin the game, some territories will already allow different levels of access. Most territories that do not already allow access will state a price at which they will open their doors—a few simply do not allow access. On some maps, the occasional territory will undergo political upheavals, resulting in the removal of rights or the ability to purchase rights they did not offer before. Likewise, some territories will occasionally offer you a deal or present you with an opportunity to provide a service or gift. This will sometimes result in being granted access, and sometimes in a considerable increase in your goodwill standing with them, making purchase of access rights cheaper. You do not need to have positive goodwill with a territory in order to buy rights, but as your goodwill standing improves, the access price will decrease considerably.

FINANCES

The final section in the Company Detail Screen is Finances. This final section is also the most important, and the most vital to running the business side of your company. This section tells you about the handling of your finances. It shows interest rates, bond information, stocks and dividend levels, and so on. The first section of the Company Book (Overview) allowed you to resign, hire another manager, and change

your company's name and logo. Otherwise, the rest of the sections (and most of the Overview) have been multiple pages of information. Finances, however, contains all of the actions you need to handle your company cash.

The left page of this two-page section is devoted to information. The first item is the Prime Rate. This rate is the same for every player, and is determined by the health of the economy. Interest rates received from cash you hold and paid for bonds outstanding are determined in part by the Prime Rate .

CREDIT RATING

Below the Prime Rate is your Credit Rating. Credit Rating is a complicated and holistic figure, being affected by a large number of factors. The rating scale runs from F, the worst rating, to AAA, the best. It is an overall gauge of your company's lifetime performance. If this decreases over time, the market will lose faith in your company and your credit rating will drop. The number of bonds outstanding also affects the rating, a higher number of bonds having a negative impact. Repaying bonds quickly has a positive impact. People will also have more faith in a company led by a trusted chairman. The five-year-weighted return on stocks (see the description of the Stock Market screen for more information) is a large factor, and one that gives stability to your credit rating. In short, the Credit Rating shows how much faith the market has in the financial stability of your company, and thus, how much faith it has in lending you money. No one factor plays too heavy a part in determining this rating. A higher credit rating can be maintained even if any one of the factors is low, or if the company has a bad year.

Since your rating is determined by your company's lifetime performance, it becomes more stable the longer you play. For example, a bond issued in a company's first year can drop its credit rating several levels, from BBB to C, for example. Several years later, though, the company might be able to issue ten or fifteen bonds at once with the same impact to the credit rating.

Credit Rating Calculation Detail

This section is for those of you who want more detail on the credit rating calculation. The primary factors that influence your credit rating are Debt to Asset Ratio and Debt Coverage Ratio:

$$\text{DEBT TO ASSET RATIO} = \text{TOTAL DEBT (BONDS AND NEGATIVE CASH)} / \text{TOTAL ASSETS}$$

$$\text{(EVERYTHING ON THE TOP SECTION OF YOUR BALANCE SHEET)}$$

If you have $1,000,000 in bonds, no cash, and $4,000,000 in assets (track, trains, buildings, and so on), you have a debt-to-assets ratio of .25. This translates to roughly AA, as shown in Table 5-5.

TABLE 5-5. TARGET RATIOS: DEBT-TO-ASSET

Ratio	Credit Rating
0 - 0.24	AAA
0.25 - 0.37	AA
0.38 - 0.49	A
0.5 - 0.57	BBB
0.58 - 0.66	BB
0.67 - 0.74	B
0.75 - 0.8	CCC
0.81 - 0.86	CC
0.87 - 0.95	C
0.95 or worse	F

The other factor that affects your credit rating is debt coverage:

$$\text{DEBT COVERAGE} = (\text{EARNINGS} + \text{INTEREST PAID}) / \text{INTEREST PAID}$$

If your company had revenues of $1,000,000, various operational expenses totaling $600,000, interest payments of $100,000, and earnings of $300,000, then your debt coverage is 4.0 ((100K + 300K)/100K). Lenders like to see a healthy coverage ratio, so that even if revenues and profits dip, you can still pay the interest. For this ratio, the weighted average of the last few years' outcomes is used, weighted towards the most recent year. Table 5-6 shows target ratios based upon debt coverage.

TABLE 5-6. TARGET RATIOS— DEBT COVERAGE

RATIO	CREDIT RATING
5.0 or better	AAA
4.0 to 4.9	AA
3.0 to 3.9	A
2.0 to 2.9	BBB
1.5 to 1.9	BB
1.0 to 1.4	B
.75 to .99	CCC
.5 to .74	CC
.25 to .49	C
Less than .25	F

Your overall credit rating is an average of the rating from these two sources, plus your manager bonuses. Recent bankruptcies incur a heavy penalty. Bankruptcy effects wear off gradually over ten years. New companies (less than five years old), take a penalty on their credit rating, heaviest in the first couple of years—lenders like a track record.

You can't issue new bonds if your credit rating is below B. The interest rate on new bonds is prime + 1 percent per credit-rating level below AAA, so be careful if you want to avoid high interest payments on your debt.

SHARE PRICE

The next figure on the left page is the company's Share Price. This is the price an investor must pay to buy shares in the company's stock. This, too, is determined by several factors, but is much more volatile than the Credit Rating. Short-term profit losses can quickly reduce a company's stock price dramatically. The Share Price is determined mainly by the profitability of a company. In order to maintain a high Share Price, a company must remain highly profitable. While debt and general financial health affect Credit Rating, share price is affected by company growth. A company that has low but constant income can earn a high credit rating, but investors want a company that will make them money, which means that they expect the company not just to do well, but to do *better than before*. No matter how profitable your company is, you need to constantly increase the ratio of profits per share to keep the Share Price high.

Share Price Calculation

The calculation for Share Price is as follows:

$$\text{STOCK PRICE} = \text{FUNDAMENTAL SHARE PRICE (ITS TRUE VALUE)} \times \text{TRADE MODIFIER}$$
$$\text{(AS SHARES ARE BOUGHT, DEMAND, AND PRICE GO UP).}$$

The key element is Fundamental Stock Price, but four factors are considered:

- **Earnings:** Basic weight = 40%
- **Book Value:** Basic weight = 30%
- **Dividends:** Basic weight = 20%
- **Revenue:** Basic weight = 10%

Basic weight is adjusted so that those criteria that would tend to value the stock most highly have their weight increased, and vice versa. For instance, if revenue is awesome and earnings are in the toilet, revenue will have its weight increased, earnings weight will be decreased.

The value based on each of these factors is determined on recent years' performance, with more recent years being most valuable—current year is projected based on the trend.

Share price based on each criteria is roughly the following (all on a per share basis):

- **Earnings:** Share price = 10.0 times yearly earnings
- **Revenue:** Share price = 1.0 times yearly revenue
- **Book Value:** Share price = 1.0 times book value
- **Dividends:** Share price = 30 times average dividend, with a big bonus for continuity (dividend staying the same, or going up year after year)

The fundamental price is modified by the trend in recent trades. If shares are being bought, the modifier is positive, and the price is above the fundamental price. If being sold, the opposite holds true. The minimum a share can go to is 30 percent of its fundamental price— further sales will not drive the price down any more. There is no cap on the upper end. The effect of stock transactions declines over time, with the biggest impact in the first six months after the transaction.

TOTAL CASH

Total Cash, the next item, should look familiar. This is the same figure displayed in the Overview and in the current year of the Balance section, as well as being displayed in the main window. This is how much cash the company currently has to spend.

INTEREST RATE

Below Cash is the Interest Rate Received. This is the rate at which your bank account makes you profit on the money you already have. This will fluctuate with the economy, but usually stays loosely around 50 percent of the Prime Rate. The Interest Rate Received is the same for all companies, and is not directly affected by your company's performance.

ANNUAL CASH FLOW

Below this, Annual Cash Flow (for cash interest) tells you how much money per year you are currently making from the interest on your cash. The figure is, in theory, simply determined by multiplying your Cash by the Interest Rate Received. However, if the interest rate changes during the year due to the economy, the current Annual Cash Flow is actually figured by the average interest rate for the year to date.

BONDS

The next group of three figures deals with Bonds. The first item is Bonds Outstanding. This is the current total cash amount of bonds outstanding. Since bonds are issued in $500,000 increments, the figure will be the number of bonds outstanding times this figure. That will not be the case after declaring bankruptcy, when all bonds are halved.

The next figure, Average Interest Rate, is the average of the different interest rates on all of the bonds currently outstanding. This is important in figuring the next figure, Annual Cash Flow (for debt). This figure indicates how much money you are losing to the payment on bonds for the year.

STOCKS

The next group of items relates to stocks. The first, Shares Outstanding, is the number of shares your company currently has issued. As you issue or buy back stocks, this number will increase and decrease. When stock splits, this number will change. For example, if your stock splits 3 for 1, the number of Shares Outstanding will triple. The Annual Dividend is the amount paid to investors per share. This number multiplied by Shares Outstanding results in the next figure, Annual Cash Flow (for stocks). This figure shows how much total you are paying to investors per year.

The final figure on the left-hand page of Finances is Total Financial Cash Flow. This figure is the total of the three Annual Cash Flows listed above (for interest received, interest paid on bonds, and dividend payments).

GAME ACTIONS

The right-hand page of the Finances tab provides a list of options for you to perform. This is where you handle financial business.

Issuing Bonds

The first option is to Issue Bonds. Bonds are issued in $500,000 increments only, but the interest rate on each bond is determined by the economy (Prime Rate) and your company's Credit Rating. The interest rate will be the same as the Prime Rate if your credit rating is AAA, but will increase as your credit rating drops, causing you to pay more in interest. Bonds are also issued with a low once-only Underwriting Fee. You can only issue bonds if you have a credit rating of B or higher. Once your credit rating drops to or below CCC, your request to issue bonds will be denied. Despite your credit rating, you cannot have more than 20 bonds outstanding at any one time.

> ISSUING BONDS IS A GOOD IDEA IF YOU HAVE A PLAN OR ROUTE IN MIND. IT IS NOT A GOOD IDEA IF YOU ARE LOW ON CASH AND SIMPLY "NEED MONEY." THE DEBT WILL ONLY HURT YOU. USE BONDS TO EXPLOIT OPPORTUNITIES, NOT AS A LAST-DITCH EFFORT AGAINST LOSS.

Since issuing a bond increases debt as it increases your cash, it does not affect your company's Book Value (Equity). It only provides you with more Current Cash (by the amount of the bond minus the underwriting fee) with which you can expand and attempt to increase your profit. Keep in mind when issuing bonds that they must be repaid within 30 years. Watch the Maturation Date carefully (covered below). The sooner you repay your bonds, the less you pay in interest.

Issuing Stock

The next option is Issue Stock. This option issues shares of stock in your company. The amount of stock issued is equal to 5 percent of the current number of shares, rounded to the nearest 1,000 shares. The pop-up window that appears when you select this option lists the number of shares offered, the price per share, and an underwriting fee in a percentage. It also lists the profit you will make from issuing the stock (number of shares times price per share, minus the underwriting fee percentage).

Since issuing stock increases the number of shares, the Price Per Share in the Issue bonds window will be lower than the current share price listed on the left-hand side of the Finances page. Shares can only be issued once per year to prevent saturating the market. Issuing Stock will add cash to your current cash amount and decrease the stock price per share. When the stock is issued, it is available for purchase by you

> ALWAYS PAUSE THE GAME BEFORE ISSUING STOCK, OR THE OTHER COMPUTER PLAYERS WILL BUY IT BEFORE YOU CAN.

or any other players. If the stock is issued while in pause, computer players cannot purchase stock until the game is unpaused. This is not true of human players. Any available shares are considered Publicly Held.

Buying Back Stock

Buy Back Stock is the next option. Selecting this allows your company to attempt to buy back shares of your company's stock. Only Publicly Held shares are available to be bought back, and only if your company has enough money to buy back at least 1,000 shares. Your company will try to buy back 5 percent of the Outstanding Shares, but will buy less if it does not have enough cash to buy 5 percent. The cost to buy back shares is calculated as shown in the pop-up window that appears when attempting the purchase—by multiplying the shares being purchased by the price per shares, minus the brokerage fees. Similar to issuing stock, the price per share is determined by the proposed new share price, resulting in a price per share that is higher than the current share price. The company may buy back as many shares as it wishes per year, provided it has the cash available to do so.

Changing the Dividend

Next you have the option to Change the Dividend. The dividend is the amount paid to investors per share owned each year. The Change Dividend window displays the number of outstanding shares and the current dividend rate, which is adjustable using the arrows to the right. As the dividend rate is adjusted, the Total Annual Dividends your company will pay each year at that rate is calculated and shown below. This rate cannot drop below zero. The maximum you may raise the rate to is controlled by the Board of Directors, who will never let

the rate be raised above the total cash currently available, but will often not allow it raised even that high.

Attempting a Merger

If you are playing in Expert Financial Mode, the next item on the list will be Attempt Merger. In a successful merger, the merged child company becomes integrated into the parent company. All property, from trains and track to cash and, yes, debt, become the possession of the parent company and the child company ceases to exist. The chairman of the child company loses his position and is forced to start another company, call for a Special Election, gain personal wealth alone, or quit.

In a merger attempt, all investors in the child company cast votes as to whether the attempt succeeds or fails. Publicly held shares appear as Other Investors on the tally. These other investors vote based on the price offered per share and the chairman with the better record, and in a fairly close race they will split, with some investors voting for one chairman and the rest for the other. The chairman who receives more than 50 percent wins the election. The majority rule means that if you own over 50 percent of the stock in the company with whom you attempt the merger, you will automatically win. If you own 50 percent in your own company, no one can force an unwanted merger. If you would prefer the cash received in the merger and are tired of controlling your company, you are free to vote for the other player and allow the merger. You can then start a new company or try to buy your way in and assume chairmanship of another company (including the one that just took you over).

When you select Attempt Merger, a window appears. This window shows a list of companies at the top, in which are listed the names of all other companies in the game. A merger can be attempted with any of them. You do not need to possess shares to attempt a merger. It only makes the success more likely since you automatically vote for your own company.

> WHEN ATTEMPTING A MERGER, THERE ARE SEVERAL TACTICS. SELLING OFF STOCK IN THE OTHER COMPANY WILL DRIVE ITS SHARE PRICE DOWN, ALLOWING A MUCH CHEAPER MERGER. IT WILL ALSO CONVINCE SOME PUBLIC INVESTORS THAT THE COMPANY IS IN BAD SHAPE WITH THE SUDDEN DROP IN SHARE PRICE, WHICH MEANS IT CAN EARN YOU MORE VOTES. IN THE BEST CASE SCENARIO, MERGE WHEN YOU HAVE WELL OVER 50 PERCENT OF THE STOCK. WHEN YOU ARE READY FOR THE KILL, SELL OFF ALL STOCK ABOVE 50 PERCENT AND DRIVE THE PRICE DOWN AS LOW AS YOU CAN, THEN CALL FOR A MERGER AND BUY THE COMPANY. WITH CONTROLLING INTEREST IN YOUR HANDS, YOU ARE GUARANTEED THE COMPANY AT A GREAT PRICE. SOME WOULD CALL IT A STEAL.

Below the company list is a slider for choosing an offer price. The offer price is determined by multiplying the child company's number of outstanding shares by the offered price per share. At the far left, the slider represents the current share price for the company. At the far right, the slider represents double the current price. Offering more will convince more investors to vote for you, and can sometimes convince the other chairman as well. This is unnecessary if you have a controlling percentage, however. The lowest price will suffice. If the merger is successful, you may immediately attempt another. If you fail, however, your board of directors will not allow another attempt for another year.

Declaring Bankruptcy

The next action available is to Declare Bankruptcy. This is a last resort, to say the least. It will decrease all debt by half. This means all outstanding bond amounts will be cut in half, as will your cash if it is currently negative. If your cash is positive, all of that cash is forfeit, no matter how much or little you have. Declaring bankruptcy also automatically drops your credit rating to F. This will prevent the company from declaring bankruptcy for many years, and decrease the likelihood of issuing new stock. Overall, declaring bankruptcy leaves little chance to become profitable again. If a company is already deeply in debt, though, it could help.

Repaying Bonds

The final action listed in the Finances section is the Repayment of Bonds. At the bottom of the page is a chart listing any outstanding bond amounts, their maturation date, the interest rate being paid on each bond, and a Repay option. Your company must have enough cash in order to repay a bond plus a small prepayment fee (which is much less than the annual interest rate you are already paying on each bond). Any bonds not repaid by the year in which they mature are automatically repaid no matter how much cash you have (or do not have).

ALTHOUGH IT MIGHT NOT BE GOOD BUSINESS PRACTICE, MOST SCENARIOS WILL END BEFORE THE 30-YEAR MATURATION DATE OF YOUR BONDS. YOU MAY BE ABLE TO BORROW HEAVILY TO FINANCE RAPID EXPANSION, AND NEVER HAVE TO PAY THEM BACK—ASSUMING YOU CAN DEAL WITH THE HIGH INTEREST EXPENSE YOU'LL BE CARRYING.

MANAGING YOURSELF

In addition to managing your company, an important part of being a successful tycoon is managing your own interests. There are two places where you can do this—the Player Detail Screen, and the Stock Market.

THE PLAYER DETAIL SCREEN

On your desk (as seen from the Company Detail Screen, or accessed from the Players List Box) is a red leather-bound book that contains Personal Detail. This almost exclusively contains information dealing with personal wealth. It's much easier to get into than the Company book, and is much shorter. No doubt your character has filled the rest of this vermilion tome with notes on other tycoons, telegraph numbers of girlfriends, poetry and other sundry effects, but you only have to worry about the three pages available in the game.

The biggest difference between the Company Detail Screens and this one is that no actions are available from within the Player Detail Screens.

The first thing you'll notice when you enter the Player Detail Screen is a big picture of some old guy. Don't worry, it's just you. Beneath this photograph of you is your name. These two items together make up the whole of the first page. By right-clicking anywhere on your picture and name ribbon, you can bring up a window showing this same information and the information on the right-hand page.

The right-hand page begins with your position as CEO of a company. If you are not currently acting as chairman, your title will read, "Investor at Large." Your personal wealth is listed after this. The first item here is your current cash, and the second is the net worth of the stocks you hold. These two items are added together on the next line to show your Total or Personal Net Worth.

If you are playing in Expert Financial Mode, this will be followed by another line, Purchasing Power. Purchasing Power is calculated by adding your cash and half the value of your stock worth. This means that, even when your cash is negative, you can have purchasing power because of the value of the stocks you hold.

Last on the second page is your Style, a description of your character. In single player, this is determined by the historical figure you play. In multiplayer, you have a chance to type whatever description you wish into this space before entering the game.

The third and final page is crucial to those hungry for a merger (or paranoid about takeovers). This page lists your stock holdings. Each item on the list (assuming you own stock) details the name of the company the stock belongs to, the total value of that stock, and the percentage of total stock you own in that company. The number of shares you own is not shown in the company book but can be found in the Stock Market Screen. The stock value is figured by multiplying the number of shares by the current Price per Share.

The percentage owned is important for mergers and attempts to assume chairmanship. Owning 50 percent of a company's stock ensures success of a merger attempt (though none is required for the attempt), and you must own 10 percent in order to attempt to assume the chairmanship by special election.

THE STOCK MARKET

Although it is inter-woven throughout the game, we've chosen to place the Stock Market section here, since it is one of the areas in which you can perform actions as an individual. In addition, the things you do in the market directly affect your net worth, and your chances of pulling off a successful merger. To reach the Stock Market from the Player Detail Screen, click on the share of stock in the lower right portion of the screen.

PERSONAL HOLDINGS

The first section of the Stock Market screen shows your personal holdings in more detail than the last page of your Player Detail Screen. Here you can see which stocks you own, how many shares of each you own, each stock's share value, and finally, which actions you can perform—Buy, Sell, or View.

Buying Stock

When you buy stock in a company, whether it's your company or another player's, you must have sufficient purchasing power for the transaction. As stated above, Purchasing power is calculated by adding your cash and half the value of your stocks. Although your purchasing power must be positive, you can purchase stock when you don't have sufficient cash for the purchase. This is known as buying on margin—outside the financial world, it's known as gambling.

If the stock price continues to rise after your margin buy, all is right with the world, and you continue to accrue stock value, even though your available cash is negative. Brokers will allow you to buy stock up to the limit of your purchasing power. However, if the stock price falls, you'll be victim to a margin call—your broker doesn't like being hung out to dry. After all, you have basically borrowed money to buy the stock, hoping it would rise in value to cover the loan, but now it's worth less than you paid for it. The only way for the broker to get the money back is to force you to sell shares to cover the deficit—this is not a pretty picture.

If this happens, take the initiative and sell your interests in other companies' stock first. Because you gain cash from this, it will bring your purchasing power up quickly. Selling your own company's stock to cover a margin call is an exercise in futility. Every share you sell lowers the share price, which in turn decreases your purchasing power. The net result is that you have to sell *many* more of your own company's shares to dig yourself out of the hole—and you still may not have positive cash, which means it can all happen again. The worst part is that after one of these debacles, you own less shares of your company, and there are very few AI players who won't come in and buy them on the open market while you're helpless to prevent it. This is a sure way to turn a good position into a losing one.

For this reason, buy on margin early in the game when share prices are low, or when you're sure the share price will go up. After all, you're the chairman—inflate the share price by having the company buy back stock from the market to prevent a margin call when you are heavily leveraged.

Selling Stock

Selling stock is very simple—unless you're the chairman and it's your stock you are selling. When you sell stock, it lowers your stock price, which decreases your purchasing power. If you have more cash than stock, then this won't hurt you as badly, but if your holdings are primarily in stock, be careful about doing anything that lowers your stock price.

Wouldn't it be great if you could perform this little trick on competitors' companies, driving their share prices and purchasing power down? Well, you can—it's called Short Selling their stock. Your friendly broker will be happy to let you sell stock you don't own, up to the extent of your purchasing power. This is the opposite of buying on margin, but it can have the same devastating effect on your personal wealth.

If you've short sold a competitor's stock and the share price continues to drop, your broker will pat you on the back and cover the difference. If, however, the share price rises despite your efforts, your broker will ask that you buy shares to cover the margin call. They are now worth more than you speculated they'd be worth, so you have to pay the higher price for them. The effect on your purchasing power is the same—you have to shell out cash for stock at an inflated price. You get less for your money, and your profit on the shares will drop to nothing if you sell them.

Don't short sell unless you are sure the stock will continue to drop in value, or you can make it do so. Of course, short selling your own stock is lunacy, but if you're trying to drive the price down so you can buy more stock, it is certainly one way to do it.

CORPORATE HOLDINGS

The final function you can perform is viewing corporate statistics. If you want to view your company's statistics, click the Corporate tab at the bottom of the stock ledger. This will bring up a screen with your company's per share data, largest shareholders, and the number of shares they own. This information is actually more valuable for companies you don't control, since you have no other way to get this information.

You can go to the next company in the list by clicking Next at the bottom of the ledger. Use the information here to tell you when a merger makes sense (if you have the majority of the shares), and to see what other players are up to in your company.

MAXIMIZING WEALTH

There are a number of things you can do to drive your net worth through the roof, and all of them are centered around the stock market. One of the more obvious things you can do is manipulate the dividend for personal gain.

Manipulating the Dividend

Dividends are paid quarterly, and fortunately, you have some say over what rate is paid to shareholders. Of course, the board won't let you set the dividend higher than the company can afford to pay, but you can definitely use it to put cash in your pocket and drive up your net worth.

Try this in December (you can do it every quarter if you like). Just before the dividend comes due—it's paid in the next month after the quarter is over—pause the game. Have the company buy back stock from the market, which will drive up the share price (your shares included). Now, push the dividend as high as the board (and your cash) will let you. Resume play, and after the quarter, you'll see that investors are highly pleased with you—after all, you just tossed cash into their pockets too—and the higher dividend will give you more cash.

We're not done yet; now pause the game and dump stock on the market by issuing more shares to drive the price down. You know the stock will rebound due to your management skills, so use your new cash to buy it up. Keep the game paused during this transaction, or a computer player will snap it up before you can. It's a bit like robbing Peter to pay Paul, but the net effect will be a positive effect on your net worth.

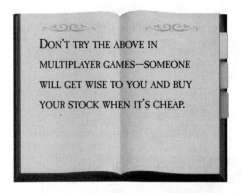

DON'T TRY THE ABOVE IN
MULTIPLAYER GAMES—SOMEONE
WILL GET WISE TO YOU AND BUY
YOUR STOCK WHEN IT'S CHEAP.

Make Early Merger Offers

When you are in a game with an aggressive computer player, use your initial capital to take them out of play early. In most cases, if you pause the game immediately after it starts, the other players will have just started their companies. You should be able, with the $1+ million you have as seed money, to make an unbeatable offer to their shareholders and take control of their company away from them.

Do this to the most aggressive player; it will take you more time to build your operation after spending most of your cash, but you'll have more time with them in a weakened position. If you are going to have to spend all of your cash to succeed, then take out a Bond first to give you a cushion.

PART III

THE LAY OF THE LAND

RAILROAD TYCOON II INCLUDES 18 CAMPAIGNS, AS WELL AS 12 STAND-ALONE SCENARIOS. ALL OF THEM HAVE DIFFERENT OBJECTIVES, GEOGRAPHY, AND REQUIRE YOU TO DO DIFFERENT THINGS TO BE SUCCESSFUL. THE CAMPAIGNS ARE DESIGNED TO BE PLAYED SEQUENTIALLY, SIMILAR TO A TUTORIAL. EARLIER CAMPAIGNS TEACH BASICS, WHILE LATER ONES INCLUDE ALL ASPECTS OF GAME PLAY. IF YOU ALREADY FEEL CONFIDENT IN YOUR ABILITY TO TYCOON WITH THE BEST OF THEM, THEN TRY ONE OF THE STAND-ALONE SCENARIOS. EITHER WAY, THIS SECTION INCLUDES DETAILS, TIPS, AND TACTICS FOR EACH.

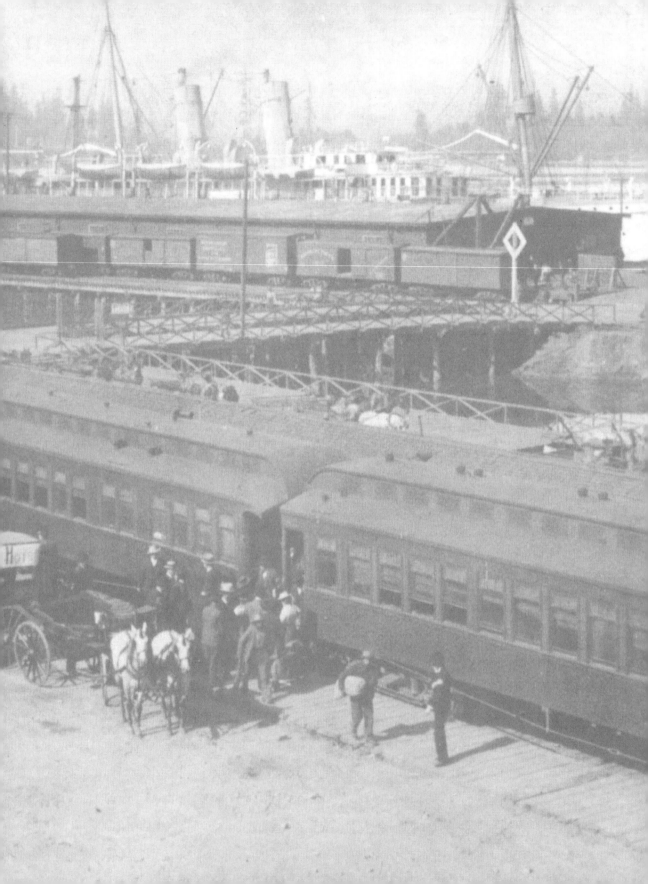

6

The Campaigns

THE CAMPAIGN MODE IN RAILROAD TYCOON II
PROVIDES AN EXCELLENT WAY FOR YOU TO
LEARN THE GAME, CHALLENGING YOU TO GET
BETTER AT THE FUNDAMENTALS AS YOU
PROGRESS. THIS CHAPTER LISTS THE
CAMPAIGNS, ALONG WITH KEY INFORMATION
ABOUT EACH ONE. EACH CAMPAIGN SCENARIO
IS DESIGNED TO FOLLOW THE ONE BEFORE.
HOWEVER WITH THE FOLLOWING
INFORMATION, YOU'LL HAVE A GOOD HEAD
START BEFORE YOU EVEN BEGIN. BY THE TIME
YOU FINISH ALL OF THEM, YOU'LL BE A FULL-
FLEDGED RAILROAD TYCOON!

THE IRON SEED

The first railroads built in the United States were a mix of old-world technology and new-world pioneering spirit. The very first locomotives were barely more powerful than horses, if even that good. However, the beginnings of a modern rail service in the United States of America planted the seeds of expansion and industrialization that would grow strong for over a century. The Baltimore & Ohio Railroad (B&O) was founded by a seven-member committee of Baltimore merchants. It received its charter in 1827 and provided the United States with its first all-steam railroad in 1835. The B&O provided passenger and freight services between Washington, Baltimore, and Harper's Ferry (powered by an 0-4-0 steam locomotive) and set in motion the dominant form of transportation for the nation. As chairman of the B&O, it's your turn to follow in the footsteps of those seven Baltimore businessmen and try to duplicate their success. Your start date is 1827.

AWARD OBJECTIVES

BRONZE	Connect Baltimore to Washington, and haul 4 cargo loads by the end of 1840
SILVER	In addition to the above, connect to Harper's Ferry and haul at least 8 loads
GOLD	In addition to all of the above, connect to Philadelphia and haul at least 12 loads

AVAILABLE BONUSES

- + $50,000
- 10% lower track building cost
- John Bull 2-4-0 available early

GOING FOR THE GOLD

Appearances to the contrary, getting the John Bull early is not a great help, since you get it in due course 18 months later. The +50,000 is...well...virtually nothing. You'll find that cash isn't much of an issue in this scenario. So, the best bonus is actually the 10 percent reduction in track cost. Over the course of the game, this will add up, but even this isn't all that significant—you'll be pulling in enough dollars to pretty much do as you please shortly, regardless of which bonus you choose.

The key to quick income on this map is passenger revenue. A combination of passenger cars and upgrades to your stations that increase passenger revenues will get the job done quickly.

BRONZE MEDAL

- **Issue one Bond**. Go to the Finances screen for your company and issue a bond to give you enough working capital to get started. Don't worry about repayment, since you won't reach their maturity date in this campaign.

- **Connect Baltimore to Washington** with single track and put a station at each end. Buy two trains—Stephenson Rockets are all you have to choose from until the John Bull becomes available—each with only two passenger cars. Any more will bog them down.

> BE SURE WHEN YOU ARE
> LAYING THAT FIRST ROUTE TO
> WASHINGTON THAT YOU DO NOT
> CROSS THE POTOMAC RIVER. THE
> UNNECESSARY BRIDGES WILL SUCK
> UP FAR TOO MUCH MONEY.

- **Maximize revenues for each train.** Set the trains' priority to red light (wait until all cars are full) so they fill both cars before leaving. Add the sanding tower, water tower, and roundhouse to Washington, plus as many passenger-oriented station upgrades as you can still afford.

Let the trains go! You should get a nice, fat sum when the trains pull into their stations. This will also award you a Bronze victory!

SILVER MEDAL

- **Upgrade your trains.** By the time the two trains have reached their destinations, the John Bull will be available. Replace your trains with new John Bulls. Again, upgrade your two stations to increase passenger revenues. Let the trains return to their original stations.
- **Connect to Harper's Ferry** and give all three stations all passenger revenue upgrades with the resulting cash from the last runs. Buy another John Bull and send it from Baltimore to Harper's Ferry with two passenger cars.

This awards you the Silver medal, but there's no reason to stop there—on to the Gold!

GOLD MEDAL

- **Stockpile cash and connect to Phildelphia.** If you let the trains run a few more years, by the end of 1834 you should easily have enough cash to connect Baltimore to Philadelphia.

Once you've connected Philadelphia, that's all you need to do to win the Gold medal—you should have already hauled more than 12 cargo loads, which is the other condition for a Gold victory.

STEEL
WATER
TOWER

SCAFFOLDING
STYLE LEGS

THE LAY OF THE LAND

A HANDLE ON THE BREAD BASKET

The spread of railroad building was nothing short of a phenomenon in the second half of the 1800's. Once the initial connections were made along the U.S. Eastern seaboard, attention shifted to connecting anything west of the Appalachian Mountains to the blossoming populations of the east coast.

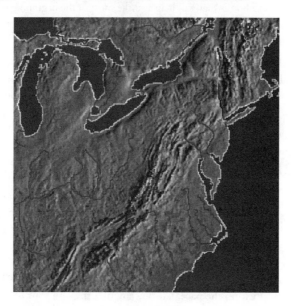

As the railroad spread west from the coast, a flurry of railroad speculation began. Over-inflated and deeply indebted railroads sprang up overnight, only to quickly declare bankruptcy and go into receivership. In this environment, the legendary robber barons where able to make their fortunes forcing mergers and manipulating stocks to their advantage. People like C. Huntington built their empires on hard-nose managing while others, such as Jay Gould, tickled the shaded underbelly of the stock market to gain wealth and power. Still others, such as Cornelius Vanderbilt, danced a fine line between the light of good business and the darkness of unscrupulous business manipulation. As chairman of the New York Central Railroad, your goal in this scenario is to connect Chicago and New York with one continuous track and haul eight loads of cargo between them. Your start date is 1867.

AWARD OBJECTIVES

BRONZE	Connect New York and Chicago and haul 8 loads between them by 1870
SILVER	Same as above, with a company book value (equity) of $4M or more
GOLD	All of the above, accomplished by 1858

AVAILABLE BONUSES

- +$80,000
- 15% lower track building cost
- +20% steel revenue

GOING FOR THE GOLD

There are a number of ways to win the gold in this scenario, but as a starting point you need to select a bonus that will help you the most in the beginning of the scenario. Since you'll be building a large amount of track, the 15 percent lower track building cost will have a greater impact than the others.

$80,000 is a drop in the bucket—it won't help you do much, and you will make that much and more with your first loads. The steel revenue bonus is tempting, but there aren't many steel plants in this scenario, and you'd need to haul a fair amount of steel for this to help you.

While passenger revenues can pretty much turn the tide here, don't completely ignore other industries. If you find a lucrative, short run, by all means exploit it.

BRONZE MEDAL

- **Start with what you have.** You have two stations already on the map, connected by track—Albany and New York City. As soon as the game starts, issue a bond to give you operating cash, then buy two trains. Place one at Albany, and the other at New York City. Set the trains up as passenger trains, and upgrade your stations with all the passenger revenue enhancements you can afford. Once you get these trains running, you'll be making $200,000 and up per trip—an excellent start.
- **Pick up the pace.** Lay down double track on your Albany-NCY route as soon as you can, and get two more trains running. This will give you more than enough cash to finance your NYC-Chicago line.
- **Expand carefully**—Remember that your goal is to connect the two cities, so don't spend a lot of time with expansion projects that are un-related. If you want to supplement your Albany-NYC operation, make sure any track you lay can be used in your future NYC-Chicago line if at all possible.
- **Link the two cities as soon as possible.** It will take time—years—for your trains to make the trip between the two cities. Plan for it by building track between the two as soon as possible.
- **Haul eight loads of cargo.** Once you have the track laid between the two cities, hook up a combination of passenger/mail cars with four cars at each end, making sure to set them to "Wait until all cars are full." They will move slowly, but they will eventually make it to their destination, and you'll receive a huge fee for your trouble. Once both trains reach their destinations, you'll have met the requirements for the Bronze medal.

SILVER MEDAL

- **Watch your finances closely.** Winning the Silver medal should happen quite easily. If you set up the Albany-NYC run properly, your company should be well above the minimum $4 million threshold required to win the Silver medal by the time you haul the requisite eight loads.
- **Don't take on additional debt.** Try to avoid taking on more debt in the form of bonds. These negatively affect your company's equity position. You shouldn't need to borrow money if you were able to get started as discussed above.

- **Manage your trains carefully.** Keep a close eye on your trains, and make sure they always go out full. This will increase your profits and result in a high book value.

GOLD MEDAL

- **Build early to win the Gold.** You don't have time for many diversions when you go for the Gold in this scenario. Get the Albany-NYC run operational with double track and four trains, while simultaneously building as much track as you can between NYC and Chicago. Supplement your income with short runs between lucrative industries to speed up the pace.

- **1850 is your deadline.** If you don't connect the two cities by 1850, it's virtually impossible for you to haul the eight loads between them by 1858—there's just not enough time left. Watch the calendar, get them connected as early as possible, then follow the instructions above to haul the eight loads and win the Gold!

> PAY CLOSE ATTENTION TO THE GRADE AS YOU BUILD YOUR NYC-CHICAGO LINE; KEEP THE GRADE AS FLAT AS POSSIBLE SO THAT THE TWO TRAINS WILL REACH THEIR DESTINATIONS AS FAST AS POSSIBLE. BUILD SHORT SECTIONS AT A TIME TO MAKE SURE THE GRADE STAYS OPTIMAL.

BRIDGING A NATION

By 1860, the U.S. rail system east of the Mississippi River was developing nicely. In the interests of opening the West and building unity amongst the states, the U.S. government passed the Railroad Act of 1864. Large land grants (over 19,000 square miles of land—more than the combined total of the states of Massachusetts, Vermont, and Rhode Island) and subsidies began to flow, making it possible to link the established eastern routes with the fledgling west coast cities. In 1864, thanks to the Railroad Act, the Union Pacific and Central Pacific Railways began construction in earnest, although both had been incorporated for several years already. The Union Pacific—headed by Thomas Durant, George Train, and the dubious Oaks Ames—began construction in Omaha, Nebraska, while the Central Pacific—lead by Leland Stanford, Mark Hopkins, Charles Crocker, and Collis Huntington—began in Sacramento, California. As chairman, it's your turn to face the unique challenges involved in bridging a nation. Your start date is 1862.

AWARD OBJECTIVES

BRONZE	Connect the cities you choose, and haul 6 loads between them by 1882
SILVER	Connect the cities by 1882 and have company equity of $10 million
GOLD	Connect the cities by 1878 and have a personal net worth of $8 million

AVAILABLE BONUSES

- St. Louis to Sacramento
- St. Paul to Seattle
- New Orleans to Los Angeles

GOING FOR THE GOLD

The bonuses for this scenario are not really bonuses at all—they are different cities you can choose to connect. Due to the different geography, it's recommended that you play this scenario three times to try them all.

The northern route (St. Paul to Seattle) is the most difficult; the central route (St. Louis to Sacramento) is somewhat easier; and the southern route (New Orleans to Los Angeles) is the easiest. Selecting a route has a lot to do with how this scenario works, but it primarily means you'll have to find different routes to accomplish the objectives.

For the northern route, look closely at the forests in the northeast edge of the mountains for the best run—turn off the trees from the Options menu if you have trouble finding it. In the central route, connect to Denver, then up to Casper, across to Reno, and down the pass to Sacramento. For the southern route, follow the Rio Grande and head west through the mountains to Tucson and Yuma. From there, you can find a nice pass that will take you through to Los Angeles.

BRONZE MEDAL

- **The cattle industry is king.** Unlike earlier scenarios, you'll find that passenger travel is not nearly as lucrative in this scenario. Focus on the cattle industry by finding the numerous areas where you can haul grain to cattle farms, thereby increasing their production, then haul the cattle to meatpacking plants. Meatpacking plants will take all the cattle you can bring them, so don't worry about saturating them. From there, find cities to take the food produced at the plants.

> WHEN HAULING GRAIN TO YOUR CATTLE YARDS, BE SURE NOT TO WASTE GRAIN. IF YOU HAUL MORE THAN ONE LOAD PER YARD ANNUALLY, THE SURPLUS WILL BE WASTED. ONE GRAIN SILO SHOULD SUPPLY TWO CATTLE YARDS QUITE WELL.

- **Coal, iron, and steel are valuable here too.** Don't ignore opportunities to make money hauling these cargoes. However, you won't find them to be as abundant or in as close proximity as in the grain-cattle vector.
- **Balance your deliveries.** You can't deliver all your food to one town—demand will drop and so will your profit per load. Spread the shipments around to maximize revenues.
- **Expand to the west, but look east as well.** Just because your focus is the west coast, don't forget to scour the eastern portion of the map for opportunities to turn a profit.

Not all your track need be connected in this scenario, so take advantage of that and turn a profit wherever you can.

THE CHICAGO/MILWAUKEE AREA IS ESPECIALLY LUCRATIVE FOR QUICK CASH IN THE EARLY GOING. YOU SHOULD BE ABLE TO TURN $800,000 PROFIT IN THE FIRST YEAR WITH ONLY ONE TRAIN ON A PASSENGER/MAIL RUN BETWEEN THE TWO CITIES!

- **Save the cash, then build your route.** It will take you a decent amount—somewhere around $1.5 million in total—to build your route to the west coast. Be sure you have enough surplus cash to invest in trains when the route is complete.
- **Load 'em up and finish the job.** Once you've connected the cities, load up a train at each end with three cars each—all set to wait until full before departing. When they arrive at the other end of the line, this will take care of the requisite six loads you need to haul to win the Bronze medal.

SILVER MEDAL

- **Focus on profitable routes early**. The biggest challenge in winning the Silver medal, is getting your Book Value, or Equity above $10 million. You need to turn a profit from the start. Look east to large cities such as Chicago, as well as the areas around them, to find lucrative routes. Also, be sure the routes aren't too long—you need round trips that occur once, or even better, twice in one year with high profits.
- **Build your entire route west at one time if you can afford it.** Once you've amassed sufficient cash (at which time your Equity position should be good as well), build your route west. Be careful to build in short segments to avoid steep grades.
- **Haul your loads to win the Silver!** Use the usual strategy of setting up trains with three cargo cars each at either end of your line and send them to the opposite end to complete the run.

GOLD MEDAL

- **Buy company stock to gain personal wealth.** Buying your own company's stock is the quickest way for you to gain wealth. After all, you control the dividend—as long as the board lets you—so buy up stock then increase the dividend to line your pockets. Keep your company profitable and growing. This will put you well on your way to $8 million in personal wealth.

- **Establish your route early.** If you're making a run for the Gold, get started on your west coast route immediately. Build short segments of track and link them to connect both cities. You can't afford to wait and build it all at once. Remember, it will take a long time for your trains to reach their destinations, so move quickly.

> GETTING YOUR TRAINS ACROSS YOUR NEWLY CREATED STRETCH OF TRACK WILL REQUIRE A BIT OF RAILROAD INFRASTRUCTURE. ON AVERAGE, YOU'LL NEED TO PLACE A DEPOT WITH SAND AND WATER EVERY 30 SQUARES. EVERY 60 SQUARES PLACE A ROUNDHOUSE ALONG WITH THE SAND AND WATER TOWERS IN A SMALL DEPOT. IF YOU RUN OUT OF OIL OR WATER ON THESE RUNS YOU'LL BE WAITING TOO LONG FOR THEM TO PAY OFF. WHERE TRACK CROSSES STEEP GRADES YOU MAY WANT TO CONSIDER A SMALL SAND-ONLY DEPOT TO KEEP THE LOCOMOTIVES CLIMBING.

SILVER BOOMS AND MARKET BUSTS

In the years 1875 to 1910, the silver booms in the southwest drew the hopeful to the "untamed West." The remote towns were growing and demanding service and supplies. Even after the first transcontinental line built in the United States, the fever for expansion and riches did not die off. Before the end of the 1880's, five more transcontinental lines were constructed. In this scenario, you'll soon realize that the booming railroad industry of the 1800's wasn't built by timid men who were afraid to take risks. It was built by visionaries who knew that the key to personal wealth lay in building and running a profitable operation. You're in charge of the Atchison, Topeka, and Santa Fe railroad, poised to dominate transportation in the west. Along with other natural resources of the area, you realize the potential for an aggressive railway magnate like yourself. You'll have to overcome nature, competitors, and a fickle market to become the robber baron that lurks within you. Stay on the alert for opportunities, as they come and go quickly, and always remember, it's you against the world as you try to measure up to the achievements of your predecessors. Your start date is 1875.

AWARD OBJECTIVES

Bronze	Raise your personal net worth to at least $5 million by 1905
Silver	Raise your personal net worth to $10 million by 1900
Gold	Raise your personal net worth to $20 million by 1895

AVAILABLE BONUSES

- +20% Stock Prices, 15% lower track building
- +20% Security, +10% train speed
- 2-8-0 Consolidation available early, +15% cattle revenue

GOING FOR THE GOLD

This scenario is a bit different from the first three. The focus here is on gaining personal wealth, which means that your priorities might remain the same—you'll still do the things you need to do to run a profitable railroad—but you'll be keeping a close eye on your personal financial status throughout.

Select bonus #2 for this scenario. The first bonus might seem attractive, but you can't ignore a chance to increase your train speed by 10 percent. That's equivalent to +10 percent revenue, so don't pass it up. The +20 percent security is also a big plus here, since robbery probability is high in this scenario. Don't even think about taking bonus #3—the 2-8-0 just isn't a good enough train to carry you to victory, so having it early is *not* a bonus.

BRONZE MEDAL

- **Stocks are the key to success.** As soon as you can, start buying stocks. Concentrate on your own company's stocks, since you directly control its profitability. Investing in other companies' stock means that you are trusting the AI to make money for you—not a wise move in most cases, at least not before you have extra cash.

- **Buy up stock, then increase dividends.** As you gain stock ownership in your company, any increase in the dividend will directly impact you financially. The more profitable your company is, the higher you can set the dividend, netting you higher net worth.

- **Be aggressive, but stress profitability.** Don't waste money; focus on short, profitable routes where the trains can make fully loaded round trips quickly.

- **Buy industries that are profitable.** Check the map periodically for lucrative industries. Make sure that you own the ones along your own routes, but expand to own those along your competitors' routes as well. This can begin to put serious extra cash into your company in short order.

- **Respond to events carefully.** Most of the events in this scenario involve an element of risk, which is not always a bad thing. However, several of the events are set up to hurt you from the start. A good rule of thumb here is if it looks shady, don't do it—it will come back to haunt you. Don't expect to play dirty and come out on top.

SILVER MEDAL

- **Winning the Silver requires all of the above, plus the ability to move quickly.** Pause the game often, and plan your real-time moves carefully in order to hit the goal of $10 million net worth by 1900. Once you take an action, pause and regroup before taking the next action. This will give you the key ingredient you need to do better than Bronze—better time management.

GOLD MEDAL

- **Taking home the Gold is a stretch.** You have five less years, but you have to reach a $20 million net worth in that time period. Be very aggressive in the stock market and look to gain controlling equity in your competitors' railroads early, then merge with them. This is a must to boost your net worth up to the $20 million mark.

WHISTLE STOPS AND PROMISES

In the first three decades of this century, steam was still king. Newer, faster, and stronger engine designs were all the rage. Presidential hopefuls in the United States saw the train as a fast, exciting, and comfortable way of covering the vast landscape in their quest to spread news of their plans and promises. From the back of a decorated caboose, the candidates would speak the words they hoped would weave the fabric of their presidential candidacy as they whistle-stopped the cities, towns, and villages across America.

This scenario is unique; it takes place between 12 a.m. January 1, 1904, and 12 p.m. January 14, 1904. Teddy Roosevelt is seeking to raise votes for the presidential elections, and his campaign staff has asked for your help in getting him to as many cities as possible in this short period. You have no other business to worry about in this scenario, but reaching all the stops will seriously challenge your routing abilities. Your job is to get to the most stops in the time allotted for this campaign. Theodore would get quite cranky if he missed *any* of his stops. Luckily, you get to set the dates and times.

AWARD OBJECTIVES

BRONZE	Take Teddy to 13 cities by midnight, January 14
SILVER	Take Teddy to 14 cities by midnight, January 14
GOLD	Take Teddy to 16 cities by midnight, January 14

AVAILABLE BONUSES

- 4-4-2 Atlantic—High top speed, terrible grade performance
- 2-6-0 Mogul—Medium top speed and medium grade performance
- 2-6-0 Camelback—Low top speed and outstanding grade performance

GOING FOR THE GOLD

In this scenario, you control the train's route and speed, but it's locked into its five passenger cars and one caboose. You can't purchase anything, although you can examine station details to insure proper supplies of sand and water exist along your routes. Selecting a train (your bonus) is the most important decision you can make in this scenario.

The only train that can reliably get you the Gold medal is the 2-6-0 Camelback. The 4-4-2 Atlantic can get you the Bronze medal, but by the time six cars are added, its top speed is severely hit, and you can forget about decent performance on any grade. The 2-6-0 Mogul can almost make the Gold, but it usually falls short. Once you've selected the Camelback, follow the suggestions below to win the Gold.

BRONZE MEDAL

- **The Bronze medal train is the 4-4-2 Atlantic.** With its poor grade performance, there is no way to win Silver or Gold with this train. Still, you might choose to do this the first time through to get a feel for how things work in this scenario.

SILVER MEDAL

- **The 2-6-0 Mogul is the train to choose for solid Silver performance.** The Mogul is the second best train you can choose. You can often win the Gold using the gold medal track route; however breakdowns and crashes can stop the Mogul well before the Gold. It's mid-range in both top speed and grade performance will hurt you on some of the steep grades in the west.

GOLD MEDAL

- **The winning route requires some backtracking.** To win the Gold, send your train to the following stops: Cheyenne—Rock Springs—Pocatello—Twin Falls—Boise—Pasco—Tacoma—Seattle—Bellingham—Portland—Salem—Eugene—Spokane—Missoula—Helena—Great Falls. There are other routes that will work, but this one will generally get the job done. Once you succeed, try several to see which you like best.
- **Check the grade overview map before making your routing decisions.** Although the Camelback handles grades well, make sure not to send it over long, steep stretches since it will run out of sand and water before it reaches the next station. This greatly reduces speed and causes its performance to suffer.
- **Ignore the Missoula event.** The town of Missoula makes a tempting offer early in the scenario. Ignore it—the Camelback can make the Gold without the 10 percent increase in speed offered by the kind citizens of Missoula. Teddy will win without their votes.
- **Avoid the long run from Cheyenne to Billings.** It takes too much sand and water to make it to Billings. Head west from Cheyenne for a better chance at making Gold.
- **Go north at Portland.** Instead of jogging south, head north at the Portland branch. This allows you to gain speed going south later, making it easy to take the hill south of Portland with a full head of steam as you continue.

CROSSING THE GREAT DIVIDE

It's 1867 and trouble is brewing in Canada. The country is tearing itself apart without a tangible representation of unity. The Canadian Parliament wants you to build a trans-Canadian railway by 1896 in order to strengthen relationships between provinces.

Started in 1875 and technically finished in 1887, the Trans-Canadian Railroad carried passengers and goods from Halifax, Nova Scotia, on the Atlantic Ocean to Vancouver, British Columbia, on the Pacific Ocean. The railroad was enormously expensive to create and presented an engineering nightmare of the highest degree. The Canadian government had to grant over 39,000 square miles of land to developers, but reaped its rewards when it was able to send troops to put down a rebellion in the west using the mostly completed rail system. As George Stephen, you must reorganize the existing eastern line to generate enough cash to finance the rest of the line to Vancouver by 1887. Your start date is 1875.

AWARD OBJECTIVES

BRONZE	Connect Halifax to Vancouver and haul six loads between the two cities by 1896
SILVER	Complete the above task, and drive your company's net worth above $20 million by 1896
GOLD	Complete all of the above, but your company's net worth must reach $50 million by 1896

AVAILABLE BONUSES

- Manager Van Horne, 10% lower track costs
- 2-8-0 Consolidation early, +10% engine speed
- One level higher credit rating, 10% faster station turn around

GOING FOR THE GOLD

This scenario is very similar to Bridging a Nation, but the mix of industries is very different. Select bonus #2 for this scenario; although the Consolidation does not give you an instant victory, the +10 percent engine speed translates directly into increased revenues. Bonus #1 isn't as effective, since you don't need Van Horne to help you—good solid management will negate the advantage of 15 percent lower track cost, and since it's a small portion of your overhead, you'll make more money with bonus #2. Likewise, station turnaround is only a small portion of a train's schedule, and your credit rating will take care of itself with sound management.

BRONZE MEDAL

- **Passengers and Steel should be your focus**. Although the resources in Canada are fairly spread out, you will find several lucrative passenger routes (such as the Jonquiere—Quebec—Montreal—Ottowa area), and also be able to turn a quick profit hauling steel and its ingredients. However, don't ignore the lumber vector.

- **Routes tend to be longer in this scenario** so make sure you have plenty of cash coming in before longhauling cargo. You'll need to be sure you have an outlet for produced resources. For instance, there are seven logging camps near Hornepayne, but the nearest lumber mill is in Ottawa. To make this long haul lucrative, haul the logs to Ottawa, and the lumber produced in Ottawa to Toronto. To get things really moving, buy the logging camps and the lumber mill to profit from this cycle in every way possible.

- **Territory rights in the United States are denied to you** in the early going, but if you can gain them through goodwill (or a deal with another tycoon), you can make some cash along the border. Just be sure to put customs houses in any station that receives cargo from across the border—this will speed up processing of shipments received.

> BE SURE TO PUT SMALL STATIONS ALONG LONG HAULS, AND BUY SANDING AND WATER TOWERS FOR THEM, SO THAT TRAINS PASSING THROUGH WILL BE REFILLED. OTHERWISE, YOUR TRAINS WILL NOT REACH THEIR DESTINATIONS FAST ENOUGH TO KEEP YOU AFLOAT.

- **Expand westward by increments.** Connect the shorter routes you find across the country to form your trans-Canadian railway. To reach Vancouver, you'll need to go through the pass near Prince George, which is located just west of Edmonton.

- **Once you have the cities connected, start hauling.** You need to haul six loads between the two cities, so place a train at each station and load up three cars completely full before sending them on their way. It will take years for the trains to reach their destinations, but when they do, you'll get a hefty fee, and the Bronze medal!

SILVER MEDAL

- **Concentrate on short, profitable runs early** to give you the momentum to reach the $20 million company net worth. Key cities are Quebec, Montreal, Toronto, and Winnipeg. You should also accept and/or exploit any U.S. opportunities to maximize profits.

- **Manage your routes closely.** You can't afford for any train to be inefficient, especially on longer routes. Make sure every train goes out fully loaded to insure maximum profitability when it reaches its destination.

- **Buy industries and make them profitable.** Buy any industry with a "lucrative" or better profitability rating—especially steel plants—then haul loads from them to increase their contribution to your net worth.

- **Watch your debt-to-equity ratio.** Don't get heavily leveraged with bond debt. This adversely affects your net worth. If you need to raise cash, issue stock instead.

GOLD MEDAL

- **Expand upon the things you do to win Silver to win the Gold.** More of the same will gain you the required $50 million to take home the gold. The biggest thing to remember is to give your trains enough time to make the run, once you've connected both cities. Also, remember that your track can be laid anywhere not just connected to existing lines. So, if you find a nice cash-making route out in the middle of Saskatchewan, it may be worth a second glance.

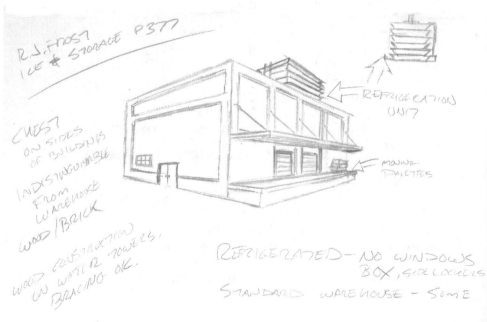

BIRTH OF THE IRON HORSE

In Britain, coal and iron had been exported from the high hills of the Welsh countryside for centuries before the introduction of steam power. However, industrialization placed ever greater demands on the resources of the British Empire. The invention of the steam engine in 1830 brought with it the method for moving these raw materials. It also brought with it men of vision and greed. Now is your chance to grab a share of that new wealth, and establish a place in British history. Your goal is to build your railway and dislodge your opponents, making you the ultimate British railroad tycoon. Your start date is 1830.

AWARD OBJECTIVES

BRONZE	Have the highest personal net worth at the end of 1855
SILVER	Your personal net worth must be the highest and exceed $10 million by 1855
GOLD	Your personal net worth must be at least $20 million by 1885, and you must be the only surviving railroad in Great Britain

AVAILABLE BONUSES

- John Bull Early, +10% engine speed
- 25% increase in coal revenue, +$50,000
- One level improvement in credit rating, +30% stock price

GOING FOR THE GOLD

This scenario requires an entirely different sort of thinking. Your goal—putting your opponents out of business—may sound straightforward, but there are several factors that you haven't had to manage until now that make it quite challenging.

First, select the bonus that applies to your playing style. Skip bonus #2—it's not worth enough to consider. The other two are both decent, but your choice depends upon what you plan to do. If you want to drive your company's profit up so you can make more money, then choose bonus #1. If you'd rather make the shares that you grab worth more money, go for bonus #3.

Whichever bonus you choose, the key here is fast acquisition of stocks—your company's stock as well as the stocks of other companies.

BRONZE MEDAL

- **Grab as much of your own stock as possible..** Up till now you've probably been happy with the salary your company has given you and the regular increase in your initial stock value was due to your skill. In order to gain the most personal net worth with the least financial exposure you'll need to control your company financially, that means you must own 85 percent or more of your stock. Once you've done this you can raise your quarterly dividend and start putting your company profits directly into your own pocket. This is how the robber barons did it, and it is how you must do it when presented with a task such as this.
- **Keep your eye on George Hudson.** Although Platner is a savvy railroad engineer, he is no match for Hudson when it comes to being a true tycoon. Hudson will attempt to buy up your company's stock at every opportunity, so make sure you get it first.

> IF HUDSON GETS TOO MUCH OF YOUR STOCK AND IS GETTING CLOSE TO FORCING YOU OUT, AS A LAST DITCH EFFORT YOU CAN TAKE YOUR COMPANY DEEPLY INTO DEBT AND TAKE OUT ENOUGH BONDS TO BUY BACK ALL THE STOCK ON THE MARKET. THEN DROP THE DIVIDEND TO ZERO. GEORGE WILL DROP YOUR STOCK LIKE A ROCK, AND YOU CAN PICK IT UP AS HE DOES SO. BE CAREFUL WITH THIS TACTIC—SHAREHOLDERS DON'T LIKE IT MUCH SO DON'T DO IT UNLESS YOU ARE TRULY DESPERATE (OR JUST PLAIN SADISTIC).

- **Place your stations at prime points.** London is a must—get a station to cover it as soon as the game starts. Place another one so that it covers most of Nottingham and Leicester, then run passenger trains between the two stations. This route should produce $200k to $300k for every train that makes the run.

- **Rob your competitors of revenue.** Later in the game when you have a bit of cash, watch where your competition is placing stations. Place your own stations so that they cover the same area, then run parallel track. This way, you can take their revenue and they can't stop you! Be careful that you don't loose more money on this than you earn.

- **Passenger traffic is once more lucrative.** Look for medium-length runs between cities. They'll net you the most revenue, but still enable you to make more than one or two runs per year, if the stations are at cities.

- **Continue to buy stock.** Don't get so focused on building your railroad that you forget to watch the stock market. Buy plenty of stock—remember, your goal is to have the highest net worth by 1855, and you can't do it without heavy investment in stocks. Raise your dividend as you gain more shares to line your pockets.

- **Attempt mergers periodically.** This is a much faster way of getting your opponents out of the game than buying up stock. Of course, the more stock you control in a company, the more likely it is that your merger offer will be approved.

- **Upgrade your stations.** Keep revenues flowing by making sure to add all the appropriate upgrades to your stations. In short, anything that results in more revenue is a good thing.

SILVER MEDAL

- **No more Mr. Nice Guy.** Winning the Silver requires that you be much more aggressive. Use the tactics above, but also spend much more time looking for ways to mess with your opponents' operations. Monopolize large cities, lay down parallel routes to steal their revenue, and sell their stock short. Any kind of nastiness you can come up with is fair game.

- **Focus on putting Hudson out on his ear.** Don't let George Hudson get a foothold in your company. As you blocked his attempts to buy more of your stock, buy up his company's stock and force him out. Once he's on the ropes, Platner will fall, if he hasn't already.

GOLD MEDAL

- **Defeating the other two tycoons is the more difficult of the Gold medal requirements.** Assuming you do all of the above correctly, you should already have a net worth of $20 million. Forcing Hudson and Platner out of the game is much more difficult. Before you invest heavily in their companies' stock, drive the stock price down by short selling. Only do this when you see that their purchasing power is very low, otherwise they will buy up that low stock and catch you in a squeeze. This will simultaneously hurt their net worth, and enable you to buy the stock at a lower price.

- **Consider an early merger with Platner.** This is a much cleaner way to remove him from the game, but make the offer early or it will cost you too much to be worthwhile.

EXCESS ON THE ORIENT EXPRESS

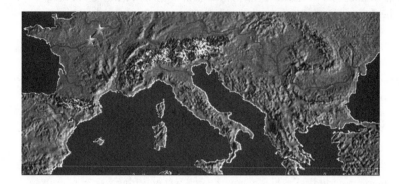

Few trains spark the imagination as does the Orient Express. The Wagons-Lits passenger cars were legendary, and the clientele were often the fabulously wealthy or notorious spies. Its reputation of opulence and intrigue was exceeded only by certain monarchies and the United Nations. What is often overlooked was that this train succeeded in providing uninterrupted passenger service across international borders. This feat was attempted for years in the mid-1800's, but the bickering of many nations on the continent made the task a political nightmare until 1883 when the Orient Express was launched. In Europe, such a feat was unprecedented in the late 1800's and was testimony to the trains' importance to commerce and the railway's importance to industrialization. As Napoleon III, your goal in this scenario is to complete the most famous European route—the Orient Express—connecting Paris and Constantinople. Your start date is 1850.

AWARD OBJECTIVES

BRONZE	Make the connection by the end of 1889 and haul 24 loads between the cities
SILVER	Complete the above by 1887
GOLD	Complete the above by 1883

AVAILABLE BONUSES

- Manager Robert Gerwig, steam fuel costs are 25% lower
- +25% mail and passenger revenues
- Manager George Naglemachers, credit rating 1 level higher, +20% goodwill

GOING FOR THE GOLD

Your biggest challenge in this scenario, as it was historically, is gaining the access rights to lay track across the countries between you and Constantinople. As you start, you only have access rights in Spain, France, and Switzerland—hardly an encouraging beginning.

Selecting a Bonus depends upon your level of confidence in gaining the rights you need. If you plan on buying access rights quickly, select bonus #3. The better credit rating and higher goodwill will allow you to buy rights at better rates. If you would prefer to run your routes efficiently, thereby driving goodwill up, then select bonus #2. The additional revenue will allow you to add cabooses to your trains, which reduce breakdowns and slightly increase goodwill by providing security and reducing breakdowns. With higher goodwill, access rights are less expensive.

There are two main routes to take to connect the two cities—one through northern Italy from the south of France, and another through Germany and Austria-Hungary in the north. The German route is easier geographically, but remember that Germany and Austria-Hungary shut down all access during the Austro-Prussian War in 1866 and the Franco-Prussian War in 1870. You can still use the route, just be prepared for the halt of train traffic. Finally, you can squeeze through the pass in Switzerland to Italy. There is a pass near Zurich, Switzerland through to the north of Italy where the grades are very reasonable. Laying the track here is difficult but it has its rewards in uninterrupted access and no added expense. The AI often builds in the south of France near Marseille and makes that narrow pass unusable do to its own traffic.

BRONZE MEDAL

- **Create a network of industry routes in France.** As a starting point, build some lucrative non-passenger routes around Paris and Orleans, focusing on the grain-cattle-food industries. Haul your food to Paris or Orleans, but be sure to balance your loads so demand remains high. Do the same sort of thing with other industries as well.

- **Build profitable runs in pockets as you head towards Constantinople.** As you gain rights, move into new territories by leap-frogging across countries. Don't try to build your route in one long stretch. Instead, build industry routes much as you did in France.

- **Use cabooses to improve goodwill.** If you're having trouble gaining access rights, be sure to put cabooses on your trains. They will improve security, as well as reduce breakdowns—two things that will bring up goodwill for your company.

- **Take passengers and mail across medium distances as you continue.** Haul passengers two cities away at minimum. This not only gives you better revenue, it also enables you to run the routes more often. Begin focusing on passengers as you continue east.

- **Connect the stretches of track together,** looking closely for mountain passes to link them together. Once they are linked, buy 6 trains. Start three at Paris and three at Constantinople, each with four passenger cars (or mail) and send them to the other city. Make sure they are set to "wait until full" before they leave, and you'll have your 24 loads and the Bronze medal!

> MAKE SURE THE TRAINS ARE NEW—
> THIS KEEPS THEIR CHANCES OF
> CRASHING TO A MINIMUM. IF ONE
> CRASHES, YOU'LL HAVE TO START THIS
> MASSIVE RUN ALL OVER AGAIN, AND IT
> TAKES A LONG TIME TO DO THAT.

SILVER MEDAL

- **Select bonus #3 for a jump-start.** If you select bonus #3, you'll be able to buy access earlier. Use this to begin your operation on the way east, instead of starting in France. This way you don't waste as much track mileage or time.
- **Use long stretches to pump up your cash.** As you head east, send passengers and mail from Paris to the current end of the line (or close to it) as you are building up industry routes locally. These long-haul loads will bring you big bucks, and allow you to hammer ahead to Constantinople much earlier to begin hauling the 24 loads between the cities.

GOLD MEDAL

- **Shave off a few years by borrowing heavily.** While your credit rating is good, take out bonds to fund your expansion. They won't come due until after the scenario is over, and you can offset any goodwill problems by operating efficiently.
- **Take the southern route to avoid the shutdown in Germany.** Since Germany and Austria-Hungary shut down access during the War, avoid this route to shave off a few years by avoiding this delay. However, this may take you several tries, as the route through Italy and along the southern coast is tough.

KNITTING WITH IRON

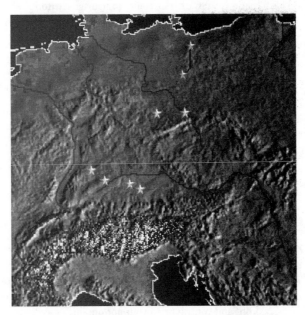

In the mid-1850's, Europe was struggling with social reforms, empire building, and industrialization. The independent states of Germany were no exception. There were rumors of a unified German Empire. The dominant state of Prussia was leading the way towards unification under Otto von Bismarck.

Involved in Prussian politics, Bismarck was able to purposefully wind his way up the political steps to a position of great power as the Chancellor of the German Empire. The consolidation of the German Empire peaked in the 1880's when nearly all of the railways in Germany came under the control of the German Empire. Again, this had much to do with Bismarck's plans, as he was very well invested in railways at the time and naturally knew what "his" government was going to pay for nationalizing the rails. Unlike current times, profiting from government connections or inside information was openly accepted and widely practiced. Bismarck collected the iron prize that became the backbone of German industry and solidified the new empire's place in history.

In order to form a strong alliance, you need to develop better interstate commerce with the introduction of a unified railway system. Your goal here is to gain acceptance from as many German states as possible by connecting your railway to their territory. Your start date is 1850.

AWARD OBJECTIVES

BRONZE	8 states connected by the end of 1876
SILVER	9 to 10 states connected by the end of 1875
GOLD	11+ states connected, including Bavaria, and 70 loads hauled in one year by the end of 1874

AVAILABLE BONUSES

- Manager Robert Gerwig; 20% lower bridge costs
- +$80,000; early access to Iron Duke
- +$100,000; +10% goodwill

GOING FOR THE GOLD

This scenario is a test of your ability to manage territories while keeping tabs on a profitable operation. The starting conditions are not conducive to uniting the states, but if you can manage to keep your goodwill high enough, you'll eventually make it happen. Note that you need to not only gain access to each territory, but you need to connect it to your main line. This means that you'll spend a large portion of your time studying and working with the Territories tab of the Company screen to view current rights, and buy new ones.

Selecting a bonus depends upon your strategy. If you like the idea of driving up goodwill by running an efficient railroad, select bonus #2 and go for it—the Iron Duke isn't the greatest train, but it was fast enough in its day. If you'd prefer to buy into territories early, then select bonus #3. The +10% goodwill is a good choice, and the extra cash will enable you to buy some more trains, although not Iron Dukes.

BRONZE MEDAL

- **Keep a close eye on your goodwill ratings.** It's tough to buy your access rights if you're unpopular. Check the Territories tab in your company screen often, and make sure you avoid breakdowns and robberies on your lines.
- **Build up stations inside territories you gain access to.** Although all you need to do is connect them to your main line, you might as well set these stations up to turn a profit and contribute to your bottom line as well.
- **Focus on "bonus" territories.** Wurttemberg, Hanover, and Hesse-Darmstadt will give bonuses to engine maintenance, stock price, and station turnaround respectively. Also, be sure to gain access to Mecklinburg Schwerin by 1865—Pasteur invents pasteurization in 1865, which boosts milk prices.

YOU CAN AVOID ENTERING BAVARIA, OR OTHER DIFFICULT TERRITORIES, SINCE FOR WINNING THE BRONZE, YOU DON'T HAVE TO DO SO. PICK EIGHT TERRITORIES, ACCESS THEM ALL, THEN SET UP STATIONS INSIDE THEM LINKED TO YOUR LINES. THAT WILL BRING HOME THE BRONZE.

SILVER MEDAL

- **Buy territory access early to get a head start.** Pay for access in the least expensive territories first, then build track toward a central point. Run your main line to that point, and you're done. You should be able to take out a bond and buy access in 5 to 6 territories quickly, then set up some lucrative routes to build your lines.

GOLD MEDAL

- **Bavaria gives +20 goodwill upon access**, which will lower the other territories' access costs; however, there is an event after 1859 that provides cheaper access to Bavaria. Wait for it, then take advantage of it to expand into Bavaria. This will make it much easier to gain territories faster—once Bavaria is yours, the others will follow quickly.
- **Send all trains out fully loaded** to meet the 70 loads in one year requirement. If you've set up lucrative routes in your new territories, you shouldn't have much problem; however, you may find yourself getting the 11th state accessed and having less than two years to make the 70 loads.

> AS YOU BUILD YOUR ROUTES, KEEP AN EYE ON THE NUMBER OF LOADS HAULED ANNUALLY SO THAT YOU GET A FEEL FOR HOW YOU ARE DOING. NOTHING HURTS MORE THAN SETTLING FOR SILVER AFTER YOU'VE WORKED HARD TO GAIN BAVARIA AND 10 OTHER STATES, SO DON'T LOSE SIGHT OF THIS IMPORTANT 70-LOAD REQUIREMENT.

NEXT STOP: THE 20TH CENTURY

In the mid-1800's, France was torn apart by revolt and social unrest, and the French people had little to cheer as the nation suffered from entropy. Still, the country had a well-developed rail system, but there is always room for improvement. As the well-meaning Napoleon III, you see this as a prime opportunity to show France and the world that you are not only a model leader, but a keen and aggressive industrialist. You intend to reorganize and rebuild the French railway into a more fitting testimony to a visionary leader like yourself, then you'll expand France's reach to other nations. Basically, you must turn an unprofitable railroad into an industrial giant that all of Europe will envy. Your start year is 1860.

AWARD OBJECTIVES

BRONZE	Total industry investments of at least $10 million by 1885
SILVER	The above, plus at least one year of industry profits over $1 million
GOLD	Complete both of the above by 1875

AVAILABLE BONUSES

- Early access to the 3-Truck Shay
- Manager Thomas Crampton, +15% on engine speed
- +$80,000, +25% goodwill

GOING FOR THE GOLD

This scenario requires you to keep a close eye on industry, while running a profitable enough railroad to gain rights—through strong goodwill—to other territories. If you want to get a head start on buying access rights, select bonus #3. However, bonus #2 is probably the better choice, since the increase in speed directly increases revenues. Ignore bonus #1—the 3-Truck Shay is no prize, so having it early doesn't help.

Take a look around as you start the game, and you'll see that you only have access rights in France. Get moving quickly, and start buying up industries, while starting your expansion to other territories.

BRONZE MEDAL

- **Make good use of the existing track.** Start earning cash soon by sending trains between Paris and Le Mans. You should also set up short feeder lines to the south that bring the various industry products—particularly the coal and iron—into Le Mans.

- **Buy up industries in France first.** Before you expand too far, make sure you control the lucrative industries in France. Once you've done this, you'll be able to generate revenue more quickly. Watch out for the industries that are losing money—some will, just be sure to control it.

- **England is your best first move.** Buy full access rights to England first—you can get them for practically nothing, and the payoff can be huge. Run passenger routes from London to the surrounding cities, and buy the lucrative industries here as well—especially those being well-served by your opponents.

- **Check your progress.** In the Company ledger, you can see how you are doing by looking on the Balance tab, and checking Industry Investments as the game progresses.

- **Take the Bronze medal.** To win the Bronze, you don't have to worry as much about profits, so keep your investments afloat. The key to winning the Bronze is expansion—buy up lucrative industries, but do so quickly to beat the time deadline.

SILVER MEDAL

- **Be selective.** To win the Bronze, you don't have to worry about profitability directly from industry much; but to take home the Silver medal, you need to check the Income tab and the Industry Profits line to see how you're doing.
- **Get rid of money-losing industries.** You can't afford to keep an industry that isn't profitable. Sell all unprofitable industries, or get track to them and start hauling loads to make them profitable.
- **Maximize profits by controlling industry chains.** If you can control all portions of an industry chain, such as Grain-Cattle-Food, your profits will greatly increase. This is an essential strategy for winning the Silver medal.

GOLD MEDAL

- **Expand Quickly.** Take out bonds in the early going to buy access rights. If you chose bonus #3, the +25% goodwill and the extra cash will both come in handy. You have to get moving—relying on France in the early going will kill any chance you have of getting it done by 1875.
- **Scout the map carefully.** Look for lucrative routes in countries you don't have rights in, then buy the rights and snap up the industries shortly thereafter. Don't waste money on buying rights in countries with light industry concentrations. Also, don't build track unless you must—let your competitors drive your profits up.

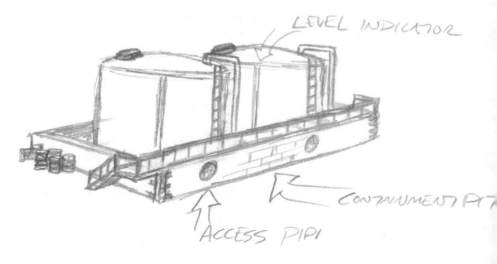

LEVEL INDICATOR

CONTAINMENT PIT

ACCESS PIPE

BRENNER PASS

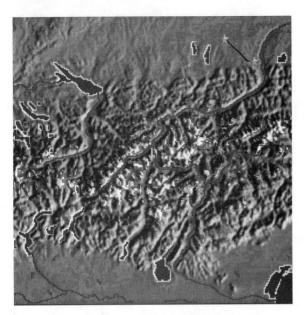

Being the bright tycoon that you are, you've been assigned the task of providing reliable service through the Tyrolean Alps. The free flow of goods between Northern Europe and the Mediterranean is your goal, but first you must figure out how to cross the Alps. The Brenner Pass, used since the Roman times, is the lowest route available and will likely be your avenue...or will it? Your start year is 1853.

AWARD OBJECTIVES

BRONZE	Connect Munich to Verona and haul 12 car loads between them by 1878.
SILVER	Complete the above by 1875, and haul 24 car loads between the cities.
GOLD	Complete the connection by 1872 and haul 32 car loads between them.

AVAILABLE BONUSES

- Manager Rober Gerwig, +30% steam fuel
- +25% engine speed
- +$80,000, mountain track building cost -10%

GOING FOR THE GOLD

This scenario tests your ability to select and construct a difficult route through some of the most mountainous terrain on the planet. The famous Brenner Pass has historically been the best route through the Alps, but here's your chance to find a better route.

Bonus #3 is a red herring—10 percent won't buy you much when you're building in the mountains, and $80,000 is not much help. Select bonus #2, since the +25% engine speed will help you all around, *including* in the mountains. Remember, you have to haul a certain number of loads after you lay the track, and the greater engine speed can mean the difference between the Gold and Bronze.

The actual Brenner Pass runs from Rosenheim down the Inn River to Innsbruck, then south to the Adige River. Follow the Adige past Bolzano to Verona. There are alternate routes in the central Alps—south from Kempten to Edolo and on to Brescia—and in west—Lake Constance, down the Rhine to its source, and then through the mountains to Varese. The western pass is the least desirable, due to an extremely steep grade in the south. If you use it, don't plan on sending trains north along this route.

BRONZE MEDAL

- **Cattle and coal will get you started.** North of the mountains, set up routes to bring the cattle scattered across the area into Munich—the only meat-packing plant around. Buy this plant to turn some extra profits. Also set up logging routes that terminate at Rosenheim—this will get you some cash now, but greatly benefit you later.
- **Look to the south for additional revenue.** Italy offers additional opportunity for getting your operation running in short order. Get some routes running hauling grain to the bakeries in Milan, as well as passenger routes of medium distance. You have the rights— use them!
- **Lay your track carefully.** Don't try to lay track in long stretches. You'll need to pause the game, zoom in, rotate, and carefully place your track in order to keep the grade optimal. Avoid laying track across the rivers at multiple points—bridges are expensive.
- **Use the track as you lay it.** Once you've connected Rosenheim to Innsbruck (if you're using the Brenner Pass), put stations at each end, then haul the logs from Innsbruck out to Rosenheim, as well as passengers traffic to raise fast cash.
- **Haul your loads to win the Bronze.** Once you've connected the cities, put a train at each end with six full cars—make sure the trains are new to avoid breakdowns. When they reach the other end, you'll win the Bronze medal!

YOU WANT TO COOPERATE WITH THE KING OF BAVARIA. WHEN OFFERED THE CHANCE, DROP PASSENGER REVENUES. THE NET EFFECT, AFTER A FEW MORE DIALOGS, IS THAT YOUR OVERHEAD WILL DROP BY 15 PERCENT. ALL FOR JUST MAKING NICE WITH THE KING.

SILVER MEDAL

- **Do it better and faster.** Winning the Silver requires that you haul twice as many loads in less time. This should be just a matter of loading up four trains instead of two, since you should have your track laid in plenty of time if you follow the advice above.

GOLD MEDAL

- **Manage stations effectively.** In order to shave a few years off your time, be sure you manage the multiple tracks coming into your hub stations (Rosenheim, Munich, and so on). If you let trains get congested, it will slow you down just enough to keep you from getting the Gold.
- **Don't load trains with more than six cars.** Six cars is pushing it as it is, so resign yourself to running more trains to get the job done. You can set them to leave the stations right after one another—just buy trains without stations, then assign them after the first group leaves.

BE SURE TO LEAVE PLENTY OF ROOM BETWEEN TRAINS—ALTHOUGH YOUR GRADE MAY BE MANAGEABLE, THIS IS THE ALPS. THEY AREN'T GOING TO ZOOM THROUGH THE PASS, SO AVOID BOTTLENECKS.

WHEN WALLS COME DOWN

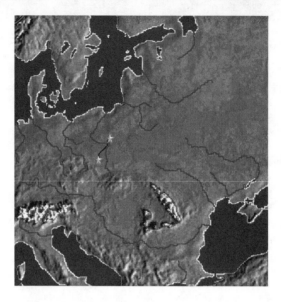

In 1991, the barriers to the people of Russia and the former Warsaw Pact nations disappeared. The demands for products and services from both sides need to be met. You are given the opportunity to earn a rail contract worth $2.5 million dollars to your company if you can connect Frankfurt am Main, Germany, and Moscow, Russia. Some territorial restrictions also still exist, so a strong showing of philanthropy and efficiency will be of benefit. It's up to you whether the pioneering spirit is born again in Eastern Europe. Once access to east and west is available, you must grow strong among the corporate giants of modern Europe. You must connect your track to existing railways, owned by you or someone else. Your start date is 1991.

AWARD OBJECTIVES

BRONZE	Build your personal net worth to $5 million and connect Alborg, Denmark, to Warsaw by the end of 2020
SILVER	Complete the above, but also connect Venice and have a net worth of $10 million
GOLD	Accomplish all of the above, but add Istanbul and have net worth of $20 million

AVAILABLE BONUSES

- -20% track construction
- -25% station turnaround
- +20% engine speed

GOING FOR THE GOLD

You should know by now which bonus makes the most sense—select bonus #3 to give yourself a +20% *revenue* increase. Winning the Gold here requires you to think outside the box—you won't get there by just running an efficient railway.

There are many ways to win here, but you will always need to focus on the financial aspects of your business. A few interesting notes—this is the first scenario in which you can purchase a Maglev train. It is also important to note that once you start, you can only lay track that is connected to your current track. Be careful where you start—a long haul early will kill your chances.

BRONZE MEDAL

- **Get off to a good start.** You only have access rights in Poland at the beginning of the scenario, but you can expand quickly within the country. Connect the industries in Poland to one another, then focus on buying access rights in the neighboring countries—Germany is a good choice, since you can make some good headway there quickly, not to mention that you'll have to go through there to reach Denmark anyway.

- **Gdansk is key to fast earnings.** Set up routes that bring together the Auto vector (Coal-Iron-Steel-Autos) and get Tires from the port at Gdansk to finish off the Auto cycle. This cycle can generate fast revenues within Poland that will allow you to buy rights elsewhere quickly.

> PASSENGERS ARE LUCRATIVE IN THIS SCENARIO, SO HAUL THEM MEDIUM DISTANCES TO TURN A DECENT PROFIT ON THE TRIPS. ALSO, PAY ATTENTION TO STEEL AND ALUMINUM PRODUCTION.

- **Watch for bonuses.** Both Frankfurt and Russia will offer large bonuses, but weigh them carefully against the cost of completion. Remember, all your track must connect to existing track (yours or the competitors'), so a bonus that may make sense the first time you play this scenario, might not make sense next time.

- **Buy stock and manage the dividend closely.** The key to this scenario is buying up company stock, and increasing the dividend to bump up your personal wealth. Be sure to take advantage of your competitors' stock. Diversify your holdings as much as possible, but be aggressive.

> CONSIDER PURCHASING A MAGLEV ONCE IT BECOMES AVAILABLE. IT FLIES ACROSS THE MAP, MAKING IT ESPECIALLY USEFUL ON LONG HAULS. HOWEVER, DON'T WORK TOWARDS ONE—GET ONE ONLY IF YOU CAN AFFORD IT, BUT OTHERWISE, MAKE DO WITH OTHER TRAINS.

- **Connect to Alborg once you've secured Denmark rights.** Win the Bronze by connecting to Alborg once you have amassed a net worth over $5 million. You should be able to do this well before the 2020 deadline.

SILVER MEDAL

- **Focus on gaining rights early.** You'll need the extra territory to expand into just to get your net worth up to the $10 million level. However, don't buy rights in territories that don't help you get to Alborg or Venice. If you have extra cash, use it to buy back stock and drive up your stock price (and your net worth)—that's priority number one.

- **Short sell and buy on margin to gain competitive holdings.** You *must* own a large portion of your competitors' operations in order to hit the objective of $10 million. Gain control by short selling, buying on margin, or any other way you can. This will help you win the Silver.

GOLD MEDAL

- **More of the same.** Getting to the Gold requires that you double the net worth required for the Silver, while also reaching Istanbul. If you've been expanding by gaining rights in countries, you should have some decent hauls that generate solid revenue. Use them to finance the final leg to Istanbul.

- **Continue aggressive stock market techniques.** Consider merging with other companies, especially where you are the majority shareholder—you win both sides of that equation. Hitting the $20 million is almost impossible if you fail to accomplish this.

> USE THE RUNS TO ALBORG AND VENICE TO ADD HIGH-PROFITS TO YOUR COMPANY'S BOTTOM LINE. WITH THE TRAIN SPEEDS AVAILABLE, YOU CAN MAKE SOME SERIOUS CASH ON LONG ROUTES LIKE THESE, AS WELL AS TO ISTANBUL ONCE YOU'RE CONNECTED.

CROISSANTS OR CRUMPETS

In the 1850's, Britain's hold on India was tightening. For nearly 100 years English dominance in the area was unchallenged. However, recent rises in Indian nationalism and desire for self-rule have provided the French with an opportunity to upset British control. As the leader of France, you are to extend French interests in India by building a superb railway system throughout the country, and thus gain popular support from the people of India and undermine English power. Access to most regions is governed by local leaders, so make sure you pay them the appropriate attention. Your start date is 1850.

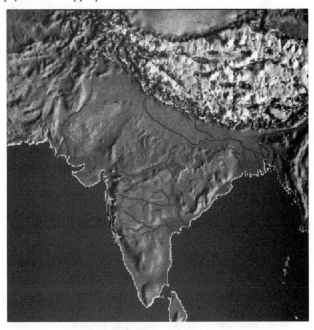

AWARD OBJECTIVES

BRONZE	$10 million in industry investments and connect Panaji with Delhi and Pondichery by 1890
SILVER	Complete the above and also connect Calcutta by 1880
GOLD	Complete all of the above, connect to Kabul as well, and be the only remaining company by 1880

AVAILABLE BONUSES

- -20% track laying, 3-Truck Shay early
- +$100,000, +15% goodwill
- -25% company overhead, +25% goodwill

GOING FOR THE GOLD

This scenario is fairly tough—the AI opponents, in particular Nehru, can be extremely difficult to defeat. Gaining access rights and running your railroad are the least of your worries—Nehru doesn't make many mistakes, and he loves to buy stock (yours and his).

Select bonus #3 here, since the -25% in overhead will really add up over time, and the +25% goodwill will assist you in securing access rights earlier—you'll need them to buy industries in other territories. There are two special conditions here as well: You can't issue bonds, and your track must all be connected.

BRONZE MEDAL

- **Start along the coast.** From your starting city of Panaji, build a line north along the coast to Bombay/Kalyan. This can be a very lucrative passenger/mail route that can be expanded to encompass Surat to the north as well.

> ALTHOUGH YOUR TRACK MUST ALL CONNECT AS YOU LAY IT, THERE IS NOTHING KEEPING YOU FROM BULLDOZING TRACK ONCE IT'S BEEN LAID. FOR INSTANCE, IF YOU WANT TO GET FROM POINT A TO B, SAY BOMBAY TO PUNE (PUNE IS AT THE TOP OF A 12.0 GRADE FROM BOMBAY!), LAY THE TRACK. CONNECT PUNE WITH SOLAPUR OR ANY OTHER DESTINATION. NOW BULLDOZE THE STEEP TRACK BETWEEN BOMBAY AND PUNE. THIS TRICK ALLOWS YOU TO EXPAND AT WILL, EVEN WHEN "ALL TRACK MUST BE CONNECTED".

- **Buy rights now!** In order to succeed in making the required investments, you'll need access rights in many areas. Begin with those that get you access to Delhi—don't worry about Pondichery. You can reach it without access rights by placing a large station just outside its borders.
- **Delhi to Ahmadabad is an example of a very lucrative route.** You can haul five passenger cars back and forth and make a killing. It's a bit long, but the payoff will usually be over $500,000 for one run. With that kind of revenue, it's easy to invest the $10 million quickly.
- **Profitable industries aren't part of the equation to win Bronze.** You just need to invest $10 million. But surely you aren't going to just settle for a Bronze win?

SILVER MEDAL

- **Add Calcutta to the mix to win the Silver.** Use this run and the one to Delhi to generate enough cash to invest your $10 million. You'll need the cash you have before this to get to Calcutta. Remember to buy up stock—you should at least be able to get rid of one competitor by the time you're through here.

GOLD MEDAL

- **Take out Nehru and Brunel early on.** You don't need Nehru getting a foothold in your company. Buy up your stock, then dismantle his company around him. Do the same with Brunel if he becomes a problem—he's not nearly the investor that Nehru is, though.
- **Use the Calcutta and Delhi routes to catapult you to Kabul.** The dollars you make running trains on your long hauls will finance your expansion to Kabul, allowing you to invest your capital rather than spend it on laying track to win the Gold.

THE SAMURAI RIDES AN IRON HORSE

Centuries of isolation had put Japan at a disadvantage when competing financially with the western world. In the late 1860's Emperor Meji decided to accept from the West what Japan felt it needed. Importing talent from around the globe, Meji set about industrializing Japan, including building railways.

As Japanese emperor Meji, you have invited the western world to help you develop a railway system to support Japan's growing industrialization movement. You will only allow one country to remain after 1912. While you've enticed the westerners to bring in their technology, you've also decided that it would be best if Japan's industry were also available to support itself; therefore you've sponsored a combination of foreign and domestic talent to help you enter into your own contest. Your start date is 1870.

AWARD OBJECTIVES

BRONZE	Connect Tokyo to Niigata, Nagoya, and Sendai by 1899
SILVER	Complete the above, and also connect to Sapporo and Kyoto.
GOLD	Complete the above and also connect Kagoshima and haul 50 cargo loads in a single year.

AVAILABLE BONUSES

- 3-Truck Shay early
- +$50,000
- +10% engine speed

GOING FOR THE GOLD

Your biggest challenge here will be the mountainous terrain of Japan—you just thought building in the Alps was difficult.

Select bonus #3—as we've seen before, the increase in engine speed is the best option, since it directly effects revenues. You don't have to worry about competition here, but the clock is ticking and you've got a long way to go. The only special condition here is that you can't resign or start a new company—if you blow it, it's sayonara for you, gaijin.

BRONZE MEDAL

- **Build short, flat grade routes.** Your best bet here is to look for short routes and haul passengers in the early going. For instance, a line between Kyoto and Fukui (large stations at each end to capture maximum passengers in the collection zone) will be a steady money maker. Build these sorts of routes all over the map.

- **Connect your shorter routes.** Link your shorter routes together to connect Tokyo to the required cities and take the Bronze. You might have enough surplus cash to attempt this all at once, but it's best to spread it out over time.

> TURN OFF TREES FROM THE CONTROL PANEL'S GRAPHICS MENU—YOU WILL NEED TO CAREFULLY ROTATE THE MAP TO PLACE TRACK OPTIMALLY, AND THE TREES WILL ONLY GET IN YOUR WAY.

SILVER MEDAL

- **Add Sapporo and Kyoto to win the Silver.** Adding two more cities is just a matter of having the dollars (er...Yen) to do it. Keep a close eye on your track's grade—steep track costs more to build and maintain.

GOLD MEDAL

- **Read between the lines and steal the Gold.** The instructions for winning the Gold are, in addition to the requirements for Silver, "connect Kagoshima and haul 50 cargo loads in a single year." Note that it does *not* say that you must haul the loads between any particular cities. This is the primary secret of winning this scenario—use your cash to connect the cities required, but haul the loads over your shorter, cash-cow routes. That way, you don't have to be nearly as meticulous about your track grade—as long as the cities are connected, you're in good shape—and you can get the job done in record time!

WHICH WAY TO THE COAST?

The Trans-Australian rail has been lain and is now open for business. As Sir John Forrest, one of the most vocal advocates for getting the Trans-Australian railway built, you must prove its financial viability. Valuable cargo from the East and West need shipping. Build your destiny from this land of opportunity but beware—your competitors will be making good money, too, and traffic will be dense, particularly along the *only* stretch of rail across the Nullarbor Plains. Of course, you get no special routing privileges on that track, valuable cargo waiting on either coast, and no track laying rights in the Nullarbor Plains. Could you make a go of it? Your start date is 1917.

AWARD OBJECTIVES

BRONZE	Personal net worth of $10 million by 1958
SILVER	Complete the above by 1948
GOLD	Complete the above by 1938

AVAILABLE BONUSES

- -20% Station turnaround times
- +15% passenger and mail revenue
- +15% engine speed

GOING FOR THE GOLD

As in previous scenarios where you've had the choice, select bonus #3—the 15 percent increase in engine speed will give you the +15% passenger and mail revenues promised by bonus #2. The increase in speed will also make a world of difference when crossing the Nullarbor Plains as well.

This map is full of half-complete industry vectors. For instance, there are Aluminum Mills, but no Bauxite Mines. In the same vector, there are Canneries, but no Orchards to fill cans with. There are plenty of Cattle Yards and Sheep Farms, but only one place to process them. In short, the only reliable cargo you can haul is passengers.

BRONZE MEDAL

- **Build short routes east and west of Nullarbor.** Use your initial capital—$1,640,000 if you max it out—to run short routes on either side of the Nullarbor Plains. Passenger traffic is the key to success, so run medium-length routes to maximize revenues. If you want to be a bit more aggressive, check out the next tip.

- **Connect to both ends of the Nullarbor track—or not.** Using the Nullarbor track is a shortcut. However, if you use it, you'll lose a portion of the revenue for every load you haul, due to the fact that you are using non-company track for a substantial portion of the haul. If that's fine with you, then lock up both ends of the track as soon as possible and start connecting routes to it. If not, *lay your own route just north of Nullarbor, but parallel to it.* You should have enough initial capital to have around $1 million left after doing so if you want to do this first—now you will get 100 percent revenue instead of losing a portion of it for every load hauled.

WHETHER YOU BUILD YOUR OWN ROUTE, OR USE THE EXISTING NULLARBOR TRACK, DON'T BUILD THE TRACK OR CONNECT UNTIL YOU HAVE A SOLID REVENUE BASE ESTABLISHED, USING SMALLER, LOCAL ROUTES. IT TAKES TOO LONG FOR TRAINS TO CROSS. THEY MAY LOOK LIKE THEY ARE WORTH A LOT, BUT BY THE TIME THEY REACH THEIR DESTINATION, THE OPERATING COST OF ALL THAT TRACK WILL EAT UP YOUR PROFITS.

- **Buy up stock and increase dividends to win the Bronze.** To get your net worth up where it needs to be, buy up stock—primarily your company's—then raise the dividend. Carefully manage this at the end of the year to maximize your wealth.

> BUYING BACK STOCK RAISES THE STOCK PRICE, WHICH INCREASES YOUR NET WORTH. BUY BACK STOCK IN DECEMBER—BEFORE THE BOARD MEETING—THEN RAISE THE DIVIDEND AS HIGH AS YOU CAN. THIS WILL ACCELERATE YOUR NET WORTH GAINS.

SILVER MEDAL

- **Buy industries to win the Silver.** To shave off ten years and still hit $15 million net worth, buy lucrative industries—especially those connected across Nullarbor—to dump extra cash in your pockets. Be sure to do this early enough to see the return on the investments.

GOLD MEDAL

- **Take it all to win the Gold.** Focus on your short routes to beef up your net worth, then merge with another company—assuming you control a large portion of its stock—that's already connected to Nullarbor. This will catapult your net worth even higher, enabling you to get the job done before 1938.

THE PEOPLE'S TRAIN

The chaos that engulfed China in the 1930's came to a violent halt when all Chinese factions united to fight off Japanese expansion during World War II. At the war's end, China's long civil war is over—the Communists have won. As Chairman Mao, you must rebuild the tattered rail system and further solidify the Communist Party's position in this sprawling nation. Your start date is 1949.

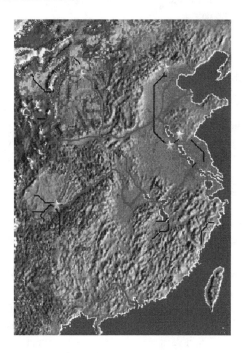

AWARD OBJECTIVES

BRONZE	Book value (Equity) of $10 million by 1972
SILVER	Book value of $20 million by 1967
GOLD	Book value of $40 million by 1962

AVAILABLE BONUSES

- -20% track maintenance
- +10% passenger and mail revenue
- +20% station profit

GOING FOR THE GOLD

You start with a Book Value of $5,072,000—halfway to the Bronze goal. The problem is, a large portion of what you have will need to be scrapped or re-routed to become profitable. Select bonus #2 since passenger revenues here are high in this scenario.

Remember, you're in a Communist country—no issuing stock or bonds, changing dividends, declaring bankruptcy, or starting a new company. You have to sink or swim based solely upon your performance in managing the rails.

BRONZE MEDAL

- **Start by cleaning up the mess.** Pause the game and take stock of what you start with. Most of what you see can be used, but you need to use some of your initial funds to bulldoze useless track that is costing you money. There are several routes in the west that go nowhere—bite the bullet and get rid of them or maintenance will come back to haunt you on them. In fact, you'll wish you could bulldoze more than you can, but concentrate on getting rid of the most useless track first. Re-route your existing train appropriately and bulk up your stations with appropriate upgrades.
- **Beijing is the best "hub" for your railway.** Keep the stations and track around Beijing and expand upon it. Run passenger trains to Tianjin, Shijiazhuang, and other nearby medium-sized towns. Keep the trains to less than three cars to move things along.
- **Upgrade to electric track as soon as possible.** With the great distances involved between major cities, you'll need the benefit of electric trains. Upgrade the short routes first, then take care of your longer hauls. Passengers like speed, so get this done as soon as you can to increase passenger revenues further.
- **Buy industries to bolster your Book Value.** Book Value (Equity) is calculated by subtracting your Debt from your Assets. Since you won't have any debt—remember, you can't issue bonds—you can drive up your equity by purchasing industries and adding stations and track (assets). Getting the $5 million you need in addition to your starting Equity should be a breeze, and will win you the Bronze.

SILVER MEDAL

- **Double your equity through aggressive expansion.** It's very likely you won the Bronze with very few stations and trains. You won't win the Silver if you don't build more routes. This translates to more revenues, and more assets (stations and track). Just make sure your cash stays ahead of maintenance costs and you'll take the Silver easily.

GOLD MEDAL

- **Time to play with the big boys.** Winning the Gold here will require that you keep profits high and invest heavily in industry from the start. Industry Investment, Track, and Buildings should be your largest assets. You can grow by leaps and bounds by buying up lucrative industries (or by buying marginal ones and making them lucrative yourself).

DILEMMA DOWN UNDER

Australia was lagging in the post-WWII economic boom. In the late 1950's, New South Wales railways were poorly run and under-utilized. You've been given the opportunity to standardize the system and reap great rewards. How does one convert an antiquated rail system using four different rail gauges and very little money? That's your problem! If you can modernize the rails, you'll be doing the nation a favor. If you can monopolize the rails, you'll be doing yourself an even greater favor. Become the key player in the Australian railroad industry, but be forewarned—you won't be able to resign as chairman, nor lay track that does not connect to someone's existing track. Everything else is up to you. Your start date is 1957.

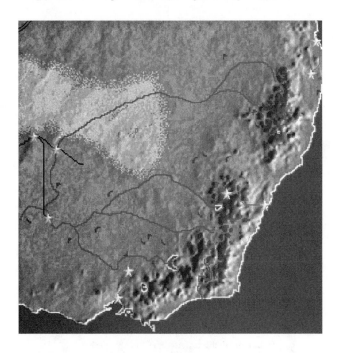

AWARD OBJECTIVES

BRONZE	Earn annual profit of $1 million for 3 years in a row before the end of 1982
SILVER	Accomplish the above before the end of 1977
GOLD	Accomplish the above before the end of 1972

AVAILABLE BONUSES

- +1 credit rating
- -25% train purchase
- -20% fuel costs

GOING FOR THE GOLD

Getting off to a fast start is the key to this scenario. For this reason, select bonus #2 to allow you to buy more trains faster, and make money quickly. There are several pieces of unclaimed track you can use, as well as your own.

There are no real traps to fall into here; you just need to use what you've learned so far, and build short, profitable routes. Passenger revenues are drastically lower in this scenario, so you'll need to kick-start the industry vectors to make serious cash. Remember that the highest dollar amounts are made by hauling loads to all the steps in a production cycle (for example, Bauxite-Aluminum Mill-Cannery + Produce-Food-Town). These are the kind of routes you're looking for.

BRONZE MEDAL

- **Start by using what you've got.** Begin by hauling wool between your existing stations at Menindee and Broken Hill. This won't be a major cash cow, but it will produce moderate revenues. Connect to the other pieces of track near Ivanhoe, and start hauling Bauxite to the Aluminum Mills.

- **Use what your competitors have as well.** Don't try to build it all yourself—although you lose some revenue, make good use of existing competitors' track. Build routes off of their track. Remember, the amount of money you py the competition is based on what percent of the route is run on their track, so keep *at least* 50 percent of the run on your own track.

- **Haul your finished goods to cities.** This is where you make the big bucks. Once you've produced food, goods, or anything else that can be consumed by cities, haul it to the nearest one.

> BE CAREFUL NOT TO SQUELCH DEMAND AT ONE CITY BY HAULING EVERYTHING THERE—SPREAD YOUR LOADS OUT BETWEEN SEVERAL TO KEEP DEMAND HIGH. BALANCE DELIVERY TIMES SO THAT EACH CITY IS WILLING TO PAY TOP DOLLAR FOR EACH LOAD. WHEN YOU RIGHT-CLICK ON A STATION, THE NUMBER AFTER THE @ SYMBOL DENOTES HOW MUCH, RELATIVE TO BASE PRICE, A CITY WILL PAY FOR YOUR CARGO.

- **Make $1 million, 3 years running to win the Bronze**. This is the hardest part, since your revenue tends to run in cycles (one year it's great, with a slump the next). To be consistent, makes sure you're running plenty of short, profitable routes. Long hauls bring in the bucks, but they make your returns fluctuate too much. You want enough small routes that they will produce $1 million with or without long hauls.

SILVER MEDAL

- **Buy industries to shave five years off your time.** Industry investment is the key to beating the Silver medal deadline. Buy into the good, lucrative, or gushing cash industries along your routes, as well as those of your competitors.

GOLD MEDAL

- **Look to the market for a boost to the Gold.** A merger with another profitable company is just the ticket to push you into Gold territory. You've got to shave ten years off the Bronze medal time, so continue the above practices, but save cash to make an unavoidable offer to another company. Snap up their routes to speed up your timetable and win the Gold.

CAPE TO CAIRO

The vast resources available in Africa have not gone unnoticed by the world. After the Berlin conference in 1884, Europe divided up Africa to suit the needs of its empires. The

development of the "dark continent" became vital to Europe's future and economic prosperity and possible unity of the continent. Naturally this didn't go over well with the native inhabitants. Cecil Rhodes, an immigrant who called Africa home, thought that a railroad could bring "civilization" to Africa. Africa could become an empire unto itself, with him as its leader. The Cape to Cairo Railway, still unfinished, is a vital cog in the region's economy. Envisioned and started by Cecil Rhodes in the early 1890's, the line covered 2,600 miles at the time of Rhode's death in 1902. History tells us that Cecil never accomplished his dream. Here's your chance to see if you can accomplish this monumental task and prove him right. Your start date is 1890.

AWARD OBJECTIVES

BRONZE	Connect Capetown to Cairo and haul at least 8 loads between them by 1930
SILVER	Accomplish the above by 1916
GOLD	Accomplish the above by 1902

AVAILABLE BONUSES

- +$70,000, +1 credit rating
- +10% passenger revenue, -20% station turnaround
- +15% train speed

GOING FOR THE GOLD

This is it—the granddaddy of all the scenarios in the game. You've learned a lot, and the last few scenarios have been tough ones. However, they were nothing compared to this one. More than any other scenario, Cape to Cairo is an endurance run that tests your abilities to do everything in the game.

You can choose either bonus #2, or bonus #3—either one will be worthwhile. Your selection depends upon your preference. Whichever you choose, you'll need to connect the two cities soon—it's a long way between them!

BRONZE MEDAL

- **Scout the north for resources and likely routes.** Pause the game and take a look around. Although industry positions change each time you play, you can depend upon a few hot spots. Lay track between Alexandria and Jerusalem in the north and haul passengers between them. There's a "sweet spot" just east of the Nile that allows a large station to capture almost all of the Alexandria/Cairo/Port Said area. This station will spew passengers faster than you can haul them.

- **Don't sweat access rights.** You only need one territory to give you access rights—the Belgian Congo. If you bide your time, the Belgian King will offer you the rights for next to nothing (relative to what he asks for in the beginning), and you can waltz through, using the British territories to the north and south to complete the run.

- **Work your way south gradually.** Don't get ahead of yourself—you need to lay a lot of track to reach Capetown. If you rush it, the maintenance on all that track will quickly bankrupt you. Make sure you have sufficient revenues from shorter hauls to support the track.

> RUN PROGRESSIVELY LONGER HAULS ON THE TRACK YOU ARE LAYING BETWEEN THE TWO CITIES. FOR INSTANCE, A PASSENGER RUN BETWEEN PORT SAID AND KISANGANI IN THE CONGO (HALFWAY TO CAPETOWN) WILL BRING YOU $1 MILLION AND MORE PER RUN.

- **Support the long route with infrastructure.** Don't forget to place small stations with water, sand, and roundhouses along the Cape-to-Cairo run. A breakdown during your "money" runs will kill your chances. Put a train at each end with four full cars and run them to the opposite ends to win the Bronze.

SILVER MEDAL

- **Start your expansion earlier to win the Silver.** Begin building track toward Cape Town well before you get rights to enter the Congo—you can run trains along this track before gaining the rights, and you'll have enough of a head start to beat the date required to win the Silver. Do the same from the south to really shave off some time—if you make it so that the Congo is the only gap you have to bridge, you'll have plenty of time.

GOLD MEDAL

- **Get the cities connected before 1895.** Plan on it taking several years for the trains to make the required trips. If you cut it any closer, any problems you have will push you out of contention for the Gold. Remember to use new trains, and support them with sand and water along the way.

7

Stand-Alone Scenarios

IN ADDITION TO THE CAMPAIGNS, RAILROAD
TYCOON II COMES WITH A SET OF STAND-
ALONE SCENARIOS THAT CAN BE PLAYED AT ANY
TIME, REGARDLESS OF WHERE YOU ARE IN THE
CAMPAIGNS.

THIS CHAPTER PROVIDES BRIEF OVERVIEWS—
NOT NEARLY AS COMPLETE AS THE DETAILED
INSTRUCTIONS FOR COMPLETING THE
CAMPAIGNS—THAT YOU CAN USE TO ACQUAINT
YOURSELF WITH EACH SCENARIO. THESE MAPS
ARE MEANT TO BE PLAYED ONCE YOU'VE
MASTERED THE SKILLS TAUGHT IN THE
CAMPAIGN SCENARIOS, SO DON'T BE SURPRISED
IF THERE IS ANYTHING MENTIONED HERE THAT
YOU DON'T KNOW HOW TO DO YET.

THE INFORMATION THAT FOLLOWS ASSUMES
THAT YOU PLAY THE SCENARIO WITH THE
STARTING YEAR GIVEN WHEN YOU SELECT A
MAP. IF YOU CHOOSE A DIFFERENT STARTING
YEAR, YOUR RESULTS MAY VARY.

BRITAIN

The Emerald Isle is calling you. With all the modern gadgets at your disposal, you should make short work of this country. Be careful not to lose control of the company you start—in this scenario, you can only start one company.

AWARD OBJECTIVES

BRONZE	Personal net worth of $5 million by 1899
SILVER	Personal net worth of $15 million by 1899
GOLD	Personal net worth of $40 million by 1899

GOING FOR THE GOLD

As you might expect, London is key to doing well here. Control the area around London, and run passenger and other industry routes out from it. Remember that personal net worth is all about playing the stock market correctly. Buy up your stock, gain control in your competitors' rail operations, then pad your pockets to increase net worth. A healthy dose of competitive nastiness is never a bad idea, either.

CENTRAL EUROPE

Central Europe is open for some aggressive railroading. You have full access to all territories, except some major cities which will need some convincing to let you in. With the ability to lay track wherever you see fit, there's no doubt that you'll take home the Gold medal.

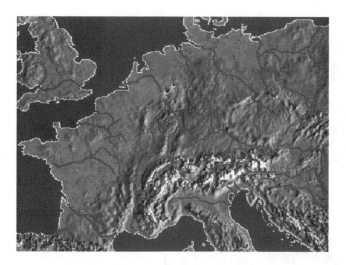

AWARD OBJECTIVES

BRONZE	Gain access to all 6 of the hub cities within 25 years
SILVER	Complete the above, but also have personal net worth of $15 million
GOLD	Complete the above, plus have Company Book Value (Equity) of $40 million within 25 years

GOING FOR THE GOLD

The six hub cities are Paris, Berlin, Munich, Venice, Vienna, and London. You can view your access status for these cities from the Territories tab in the company ledger, just as you would view any country's status, and you buy their access rights the same way. Each one charges $500,000 for access rights, so you'll need a total of $3 million to gain the access you need to win the Bronze. Taking home the Gold requires you to both manage your stock portfolio well, and keep grabbing assets for the company. Don't get so hung up on accessing the six cities that you forget to run your railroad properly—you'll need plenty of short, profitable routes.

CHINA

In this scenario, you're free to build your railway empire in the home of some of the world's oldest civilizations—China. There are no limitations placed upon you, so construct your railroad dynasty in any way you choose.

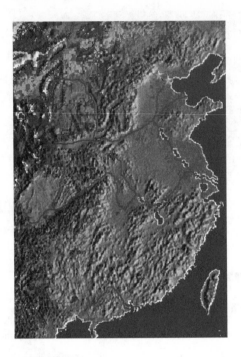

AWARD OBJECTIVES

BRONZE	Personal net worth of $7 million within 35 years
SILVER	Personal net worth of $20 million within 35 years
GOLD	Personal net worth of $35 million within 35 years, and connect Beijing to Zhanjiang.

GOING FOR THE GOLD

Beijing should be a major hub in your railway expansion—haul passengers to all the nearby cities, and be sure to put a station at Tianjin to take advantage of the ports that are most likely there. There are plenty of industries located in and around city clusters throughout China. You shouldn't need to resort to long hauls, except for the one between Beijing and Zhanjiang. The mountains make that connection tough, but for the purpose of winning the Gold, you don't have to run trains across it—just connect the cities as best as you can to win the Gold.

EASTERN USA

The American Eastern seaboard is ripe for the picking. You have the potential to become a living legend. In the 19th century, the United States wasn't called the "Land of Opportunity" for nothing!

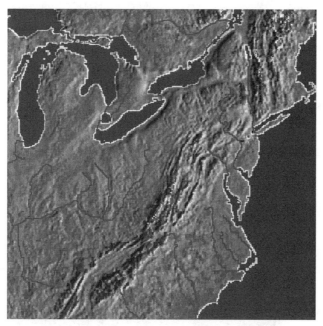

AWARD OBJECTIVES

BRONZE	Highest personal net worth in 25 years
SILVER	Complete the above plus have the most loads hauled
GOLD	Add company book value (equity) of $40 million to the above requirements

GOING FOR THE GOLD

You can make more cash faster by focusing your efforts in large cities along the coast—New York, Philadelphia, Baltimore/Washington, D.C. In addition, you can connect to Chicago and Detroit to drive up revenues—a route between Chicago and New York was the first major expansion that served as a springboard for the railroad across the rest of the nation. Buy back stock, raise your dividend, and invest heavily in competitors to grow your net worth, but be careful—if a competitor with a higher net worth has a stake in your company, driving up the stock price or dividend can backfire since it will benefit them as well. To win the Gold, you'll need to merge with your competitors, since it's unlikely that you can get enough assets on your own to reach a $40 million book value.

KOREA

If Korea had not suffered the pains of civil war in 1950, along with the subsequent split between north and south, what would it have done? How would you shape its industrial destiny with your railway? This scenario gives you the entire Korean peninsula to work with and see what you can do.

AWARD OBJECTIVES

BRONZE	Company book value of $20 million by 1970
SILVER	Accomplish the above, plus connect Pusan to Ch'ongjin
GOLD	Complete both of the above objectives, plus haul 80 loads of cargo in one year

GOING FOR THE GOLD

Winning the Gold here requires that you build short, profitable routes all over the country. Seoul is a great hub, but you can do just as well on the other side of the country. Work the coastlines to avoid track laying hardships, and haul any cargo you can get. Passengers provide decent revenue, but there are plenty of industries to choose from as well. Buy good industries and continue to expand to keep book value high. Complete the 80 loads objective by using several short routes—the ones that can be traversed 4 times per year by one train—and keeping trains under 4 cars for speed.

NORTH AMERICA

Bursting with opportunity, North America awaits your railway vision. With no borders to hinder your expansion, you can mold the entire continent into your own personal money machine.

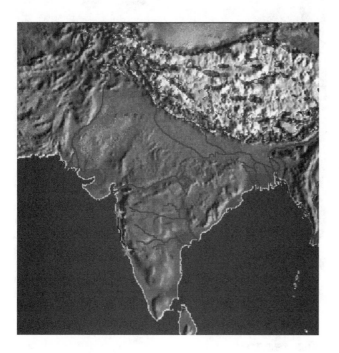

AWARD OBJECTIVES

BRONZE	None
SILVER	None
GOLD	None

GOING FOR THE GOLD

There are no objectives here, so dive in and have fun. Try your hand at linking Canadian and U.S. cities, and Mexico—do something different. It's all for fun in this scenario, so get to it!

SCANDINAVIA

The rugged landscape of Scandinavia presents many challenges. Fight against the terrain and your competitors to dominate this scenario. There are plenty of industries available, so take a good look around before you start.

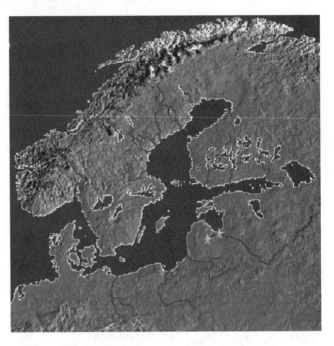

AWARD OBJECTIVES

BRONZE	Company book value of $15 million within 25 years
SILVER	In addition to the Bronze requirements, connect Norway to Germany
GOLD	Accomplish all of the above, and haul 100 car loads in one year

GOING FOR THE GOLD

A great place to start in this scenario is the Stockholm area. With Uppsala, Vasteras, Orebro and Linkoping nearby, you'll be able to get things rolling in no time. Remember that book value is calculated by subtracting your debt from assets, so stay ahead of the curve by aggressive expansion (more track and stations) and industry investment. Norway is the northernmost country in Scandinavia, with the most mountainous terrain. Connect it to a German town, but don't worry about the grade in the mountains—you don't have to haul anything over this route.

SOUTH AMERICA

The vast continent of South America is your playground in this scenario—make the most of it by carefully watching your track costs, especially when building in the jungle. You've got company here—Clement Attlee and Henckel von Donnersmarck—so keep an eye on them, or they'll steal you blind.

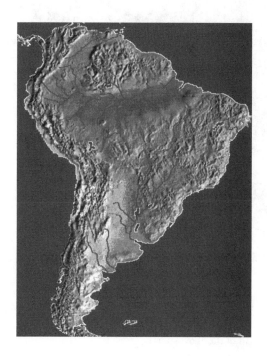

AWARD OBJECTIVES

BRONZE	Highest personal net worth after 30 years
SILVER	Same as above, but net worth must be over $20 million
GOLD	Same as above, but net worth must be over $50 million

GOING FOR THE GOLD

Look along the coastline for easy profits early. You don't have to connect all your track, so once you have a good start—say in the Rio-Sao Paulo area—work your way inland. You don't have to worry about access rights, so keep expanding. Keep a close eye on your stock, and buy as much of it as you can. Drive the dividend up, and invest in your competitors' companies. To reach $50 million, you'll need to merge with the other two companies and keep them out of yours. If one of them gets a foothold in your company, drive them out by temporarily dropping the dividend or issuing stock.

SOUTHERN USA

The early days of industrial growth in the south were both exciting and troubled. You must make your living here, and build a railroad empire that becomes the envy of the north.

AWARD OBJECTIVES

BRONZE	Highest personal net worth at the end of 30 years
SILVER	Accomplish the above, plus book value of at least $20 million
GOLD	All of the above, plus control at least 70 percent of the existing track on the map

GOING FOR THE GOLD

As it was historically, agriculture is the key to winning here. Haul grain to cattle yards and bakeries, then haul the food to cities to make serious cash. You can make good revenue from passengers, so be sure to upgrade your stations to maximize passenger revenues. Look along the eastern seaboard—Washington, D.C., is a key area for you to connect to. You'll need to merge with competitors to make sure you meet the Gold medal requirements.

THE MEDITERRANEAN

Southern Europe was slow to embrace the Iron Horse. Carve your name on this historic region, and show the world who is king of the Iron Highway.

AWARD OBJECTIVES

BRONZE	Personal net worth of $5 million in 25 years
SILVER	Accomplish the above, plus have highest lifetime loads hauled
GOLD	Book value of at least $55 million, in addition to the above

GOING FOR THE GOLD

This scenario requires you to do it all, and do it flawlessly. If you plan to reach Gold medal status here, you've got to gain control of your stock and drive your net worth up, run a high-load, short distance operation (more loads rather than higher revenues), and you must be sure you invest in enough industries as well. It's imperative that you take over your opponents' companies—this will usually insure a Silver win, and possibly catapult you to Gold. Watch your book value closely, and avoid issuing bonds if at all possible.

UNITED STATES

The United States lies waiting for a successful railway. You have plenty of room to expand, and hopefully the tools to do so. In this scenario, you have to stick with the first company you start, since you won't be able to start a second.

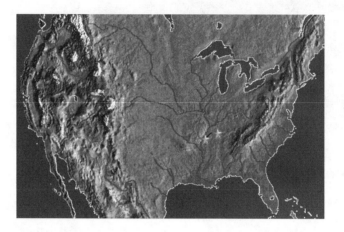

AWARD OBJECTIVES

BRONZE	Personal net worth of $10 million within 35 years
SILVER	Accomplish the above, plus have a book value of $30 million
GOLD	Personal net worth, and book value of at least $50 million

GOING FOR THE GOLD

You have plenty of area to cover, so this one should be a bit easier. Concentrate on passengers, but also on the auto vector and on owning complete vectors to pump up production. Set up several medium-length routes at the start, and expand around them. Distribute loads effectively to keep demand high, which directly relates to profits. Perform the usual magic to drive up the dividend o stock you own and increase your net worth. Remember that dividends are paid in January, so buy up stock in December, drive the price up by having the company buy stock back in the same month, then pump up the dividend to astronomical levels before year end. Then use the cash you gain to buy more stock—once you've driven stock prices down by issuing more shares. Hey, it's no nice, but now you know where the term "Robber Baron" came from. Best of all, it won't affect you book value.

WESTERN USA

This scenario will play a bit differently than the previous U.S. map, since you start 40 years earlier (unless you change the start date). Your playground is everything west of the Mississippi.

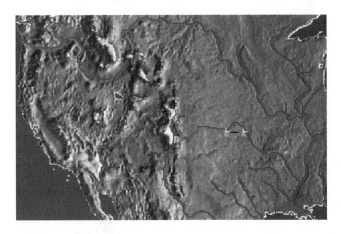

AWARD OBJECTIVES

BRONZE	$5 million net worth within 20 years
SILVER	Accomplish the above and gain a company net worth of $40 million
GOLD	All of the above plus haul 120 loads of cargo in one year

GOING FOR THE GOLD

Again, this is a scenario that requires you to be aggressive. Start with short, profitable routes that you can haul multiple trains on per year, and expand with long hauls to maximize the big hits. Use all the tricks you've learned, since your timeframe has compressed to 20 years! That means that by 1880, you have to build what actually took some 80 years to build. Good luck—this one's a real challenge.

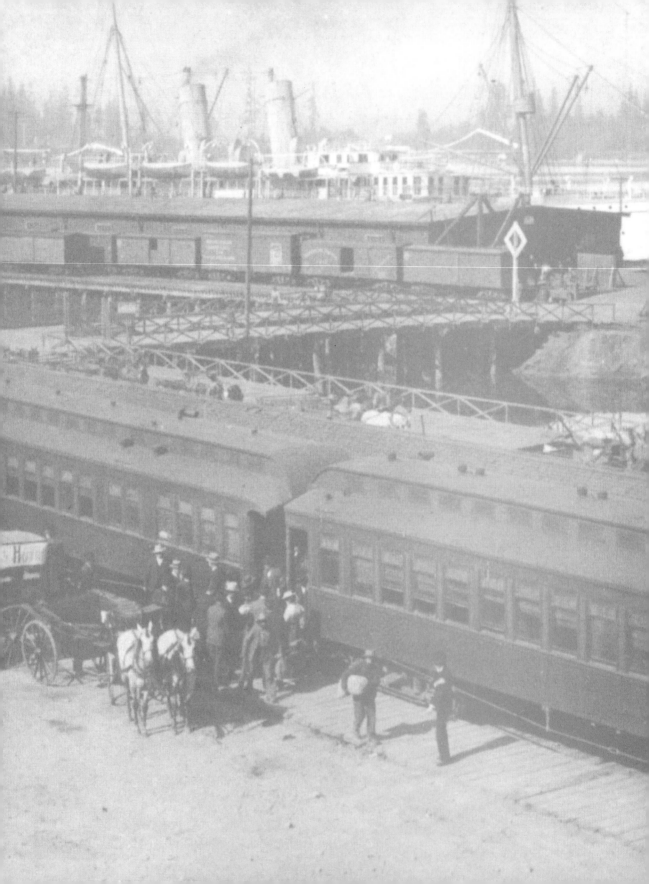

PART IV

RUNNING WITH THE BIG DOGS

YOU'VE PLAYED THE COMPUTER AND YOU COMPLETED THE CAMPAIGN SCENARIOS. YOU TOOK HOME SOME BRONZE MEDALS, MAYBE EVEN A FEW SILVER AND GOLD. MAYBE YOU EVEN PLAYED YOUR LITTLE BROTHER, HUMILIATED HIM, AND YOU THOUGHT YOU WERE KING OF THE HILL. THEN YOU JUMPED INTO THE MIDDLE OF A REAL MULTIPLAYER GAME, AND GOT SHUFFLED TEN WAYS FROM SUNDAY. AND HERE YOU SIT, POOR, BANKRUPT, COLD, AND PLAYER #3 CONTROLS YOUR COMPANY. THINK THIS WILL NEVER HAPPEN TO YOU? WELL, BAD NEWS. EVENTUALLY, IT WILL HAPPEN. THIS SECTION IS HERE TO BEEF YOU UP AND HAVE YOU GOING FOR THE JUGULAR. SOON, YOU'LL BE TOP DOG. LEADER OF THE PACK. KING OF THE JUNKYARD. THE BIG KAHUNA. ALL YOU NEED TO DO IS READ ON.

Welcome to the Neighborhood

CHANCES ARE YOU HAVE A DECENT HANDLE

ON PLAYING THE GAME, BUT IF YOU HAVEN'T

PLAYED IT AGAINST OTHER PEOPLE, YOU'RE IN

FOR A SURPRISE. RAILROAD TYCOON II

MULTIPLAYER GAMES ARE UNIQUE, GIVING YOU

THE CHANCE TO LIE, CHEAT, STEAL, AND

OTHERWISE DO ALL SORTS OF NASTY THINGS

TO YOUR FRIENDS. THIS IS ECONOMIC WARFARE

AT ITS FINEST.

MULTIPLAYER BASICS

This chapter is structured a bit differently than previous ones. We've put together several suggestions for multiplayer games and outlined them below. Rather than spend time telling you how to set up a multiplayer game (which is covered very well in the User Manual), we wanted to spend our time here discussing multiplayer tactics.

There are two big changes between Multiplayer games and that tame creature you know as the Campaign mode. In Multiplayer games:

- **Real dogs bite.** You're playing against real people. People that know as much as you do, and probably more. They won't be making the mistakes that the computer does, and they won't be shy about expanding when you don't.

- **Time moves differently.** In the single-player experience, you could pause the game and take half an hour to find your routes, lay them out, set them up, and get them going. Once you had done that, you could crank the speed up to 10 and let the money roll in until you had enough to hit Pause again. When you went into the stock market screen, the game paused and you could survey your choices, knowing they were as safe as the trains paused in the main window. In Multiplayer, things change quite a bit. Now, time marches on, no matter which screen you are in. Every player can adjust the speed of the game, which means that any time you panic and pause the game, another player can un-pause it again. And even when the game is paused, other players can buy stocks and plant stations right under your nose. The multiplayer experience calls for quick actions, and non-stop activity.

The only feature in multiplayer games that is not in regular single-player mode is the Chat function. Hit the TAB key and type in messages (taunts, whatever) to the other players. Get a psychological hand up on them, but keep it fun. You can't win if they quit the game from frustration.

Following are some general tips for multiplayer games. Everyone has their own style, so pick the tips that fit yours, and try to use these to help you come up with your own.

HIT THE GROUND RUNNING

As in most multiplayer games, the key to winning is getting everything going at the beginning of the game. With so many variables, it's important that you focus and get the job done early.

- **Get off to a quick start.** A large part of the outcome in a multiplayer game will be decided near the beginning. The few players that find the best starting locations at the beginning are the ones that will set up the firmest foundations. They will make the most money for expansion, and more quickly, so they can jump on that next good route you have your eye on. The two or three players that find the best starting locations will almost always be the ones fighting for control at the end, while the others will have sickly, weak companies, or will have lost their companies in a merger to one of the Big Guys.

- **Delay is a killer**. Find a route quickly, and set it up. Once you know where you want your station to be, put one there. Don't bother laying track first—it takes too long. Your starting locations (or at least one of them) will almost always be in large cities. If this is the case, try your best to make those stations large ones. Take up all of the space you can in there, and crowd your opponents out. Take out a bond (or two if you can) to set up a good first route—it will pay off later.

- **Work the market.** As soon as you can spare the time (if not sooner) start looking for stocks. Almost everyone will make a decent start. So while stock prices start low (read: when you can afford them), you can bet that they will go up quickly, making you lots of cash.

BITE IN AND HOLD ON

Establishing your position is one thing, but keeping it is another. You'll have to fight every step of the way to keep other players from taking over the hold you've established.

- **Expansion is the key.** Once you've claimed your place, keep it. Constantly expand. This means playing close to the wire. If you have a route in mind, save up for it. Otherwise, use as much money as you can to become as efficient and profitable as possible.

- **Don't waste money; make every expenditure count**. You should never look over at your company cash and wonder what to do with that two million you suddenly have. You should never have that much (unless you just finished a *really* good run), and you should never wonder when it does happen. You should automatically start further expansion. That might mean extending your route. It might mean buying back stock to drive your stock share price up. It might mean buying industries. Or it might simply mean getting around to paying back those bonds you owe.

- **Invest in your competitors**. An excellent way to both expand your empire and scare your competitors is to buy up shares of their stock. Nothing is worse than checking your company's stock and finding out that you are no longer the majority shareholder!

> BUYING INDUSTRIES REQUIRES KEEPING AN EYE ON THOSE SERVICED BY OTHER PLAYERS AS WELL AS YOURSELF. YOU CAN TRY TO PLAY THE ODDS AND BUY INDUSTRIES UP BEFORE THEY BECOME PROFITABLE IN THE HOPES THAT THE OTHER PLAYER WILL SERVICE THEM ENOUGH TO MAKE YOU MONEY. OR YOU CAN GO THE MORE CONSERVATIVE ROUTE AND KEEP A SHARP EYE OUT FOR THAT BAKERY OR TEXTILE MILL THAT SUDDENLY BECOMES LUCRATIVE. OR TRY THE OPPOSITE STRATEGY. LET PLAYERS "WASTE" THEIR MONEY BUYING UP YOUR INDUSTRIES WHILE YOU USE YOUR MONEY TO EXPAND AND CREATE PROFITABLE RUNS. SO MANY CHOICES, SO LITTLE TIME...

- **Borrow to finance expansion.** Bonds aren't your enemies. They will only hurt you when you neglect them, or when you issue so many that you are spending all of your revenue on interest. Use them wisely, but don't be afraid to use them. Taking out three bonds to try to come out of the hole or set up a mediocre route will usually hurt you. But using that money to set up a great route can set you so far ahead of your competitors early in the game and send you on a smooth course to a win.

IT'S A DOG-EAT-DOG WORLD

In Multiplayer more than anywhere else, nice guys finish last. You've got to be aggressive and get the things you need—especially if someone else has them.

- **Stealing from other players is a must for good multiplayer tycoons.** Human players have better control than computer players, so setting up stations and parallel routes along theirs won't work as well. But big cities can be a deciding factor, so you can rarely afford to let other players monopolize their use. The big cities usually make enough for two players, and have the most demand for goods and food. So even if another player is set inside the metropolis you dream for, feel free to set your own station down in a spot that covers as much as you can manage.
- **Hit 'em where it hurts.** If your competition is making food at a bakery that happens to be covered by your station as well, use it! Let the other player do the hard work (and less profitable) while you steal as much food as you can from them and make the big bucks. Remember, it's first come first serve.

> A NOTE ON UPGRADING YOUR STATIONS. IN MULTIPLAYER, YOU USUALLY DO NOT WANT TO GIVE ALL POSSIBLE PASSENGER UPGRADES TO YOUR STATIONS. THE HOTELS AND SALOONS MAKE A GOOD BIT OF EXTRA CASH, BUT EXPANSION IS USUALLY BETTER IN THE FAST-PACED WORLD OF MULTIPLAYER GAMES. GO BACK AND PUT IN WHAT YOU CAN WHEN YOU HAVE EXTRA CASH, BUT NOT WHEN YOU ONLY HAVE ENOUGH TO SET UP THAT EXTRA ROUTE.

MULTIPLAYER MAPS

Even the best players will tell you that going into a game without knowing your surroundings is, at best, a losing cause. Fortunately, you've already had the chance to play each of the game's multiplayer maps—they're the same as the stand-alone scenarios. Although the maps are identical, a few tips for each map won't hurt your chances of coming away with a victory.

> THE MEDAL REQUIREMENTS WON'T AFFECT YOUR PLAY, BUT MAKE SURE YOU'VE PLAYED THROUGH THE SCENARIOS IN SINGLE-PLAYER MODE FIRST SO YOU ARE FAMILIAR WITH THE MAP.

BRITAIN

To dominate Britain, make your move early. Dominate the southern coastline, setting up short routes from London down the coast to Maidstone and Brighton, then head west along the coast. There's enough here to keep you busy for awhile, with Birmingham and areas surrounding it as your next step.

CENTRAL EUROPE

As in the single-player game, you don't have access rights in the six key cities, but that shouldn't stop you from moving things along quickly. Of course, you can and should fudge a bit by placing track and stations on the borders of the taboo cities to collect their cargoes anyway. This is a quick way to beat your competition to these cities and rake in the cash.

CHINA

Don't ignore Taiwan—a route on the island between T'aipei and Kaohsiung can easily net you a fortune from passenger traffic early in the game. Beyond that, stick to the coast as much as possible—the interior consists of too many long, dry stretches for you to go there first.

EASTERN USA

If you live in the United States, then your starting point is obvious—control of the Eastern seaboard will win the game for you. However, don't depend on passenger revenues to get the job done. Support the steel industry and expand your empire to reach Chicago. All your track must connect in this scenario, so expansion is a bit tougher here.

KOREA

The terrain in Korea is your biggest challenge. If you get going fast enough, you can lock up valuable routes, forcing competitors to use your track rather than build track with unmanageable grades. Industry is sparse in Korea, so this is likely to degenerate into an all out stock market slugfest in a hurry—make sure you have a solid position in your company, and a good foothold in the others before the shares hit the fan.

NORTH AMERICA

As in the United States, the Canadian eastern coastline is a lucrative place to start, and most players won't think to go there first. Montreal, Ottawa, Toronto—own these Canadian markets in particular, in addition to the usual U.S. ones. The late default start date on this map guarantees some serious competition in this huge area.

SCANDANAVIA

The Scandinavian peninsula is a small playground, so don't bring a ton of people to the party or things will get nasty too quick. Make sure you start some routes in Germany soon, and expand south from there. There are some decent medium hauls for passenger revenue (Hamburg to Berlin) as well as several coal mines near Hamburg's twin steel mills. Exploit this area as you expand.

SOUTH AMERICA

As in the other mountainous scenarios, stick to the coast in the early going. There's a massive port complex near Natal—build routes south along the coast from Natal to dig in quick. Control the cattle market as much as possible, as well as any other good or better businesses.

SOUTHERN USA

Own plenty of industries, and haul passengers at least medium distances to show high profits here. Do your best to set up complete industry circuits that you own. Don't forget, Washington D.C. is on the map, as is New Orleans. Control both of them, and invest heavily in the market to drive your competitors out of the country one-by-one.

THE MEDITERRANEAN

Terrain will be a bit of a problem in this scenario—lock up valuable routes by getting your track there first. Or, as an alternative, let others lay the track while you snap up their stock, then use their track until you can afford a merger. Northern Italy is usually very rich in industry, and you can do well building in Germany and on to the east as well.

UNITED STATES

Use the same strategies you used in North America to build a sprawling empire as soon as you can. This should be familiar territory—industry and passengers are a necessary mix on this sprawling map. Autos will be another solid producer, and don't neglect ports as depots. There are enough open spaces to allow you to steal from your neighbors by placing stations in the same collection zone as their own.

WESTERN USA

The default starting date is a bit early, so passenger revenues will soar until around 1900 or so—make the most of this. Watch the industry mix closely, and set yourself up to benefit from the auto vector when it appears. Tight control of ports will also help you win the day here.

PART V

CREATING YOUR OWN PLAYGROUNDS

WHILE PLAYING *RAILROAD TYCOON II,* HAVE YOU FOUND YOURSELF WONDERING HOW THINGS REALLY WORK? HAVE YOU WISHED YOU COULD BUILD YOUR OWN SCENARIOS AND TEST YOUR ABILITY TO RECREATE A HISTORICAL PERIOD, OR CREATE SOMETHING COMPLETELY NEW? IF SO, THEN THIS SECTION IS FOR YOU. WITH DETAILED INFO ON THE MAP EDITOR INCLUDED WITH THE GAME, AS WELL AS A PRIMER ON USING THE EVENT EDITOR—THE HEART OF MAKING REALISTIC SCENARIOS. SO DIVE IN, AND DISCOVER WHAT IT'S LIKE TO RECREATE HISTORY—LITERALLY.

The Map Editor

THIS CHAPTER IS DEVOTED TO A BRIEF INTRO

TO THE MAP EDITOR THAT'S INCLUDED WITH

THE GAME. IT IS NOT INTENDED TO BE AN

EXHAUSTIVE REFERENCE, BUT MERELY TO GET

YOU FAMILIAR WITH COMMANDS AND GET YOU

STARTED.

CREATING A NEW MAP

To master the art of map-making, you need to first be familiar with the terrain you are trying to replicate. Whether real or fantasy, knowing as much as you can before you begin will make the job go smoothly and worry-free. Don't expect it to be perfect the first time though, particularly if you attempt a large map. In fact, you should stick to a smaller map until you are familiar with the editor, and are ready for a larger project.

To create a new map, follow these steps:

1 From the main introduction screen press the **Editor** button.

2 Select **New Map**.

3 The width and height sliders will determine the size of your map in a grid overlay, not the maximum total in polygons. Your total should not exceed 125,000 unless you have more than 16MB of RAM. Again, stick with something small to start with.

4 There are two ways to continue from here. You can either create your map *From Scratch* or import your map *From Image.* If you choose to create your map *From Scratch,* you'll go straight into the editor mode with a flat grassy area the size you specified. Now just run through the different buttons on the left side to "paint in" terrain or pull the terrain into the shape you want—we'll go over each button a little later.

If your file will be imported *From Image,* you'll be given a dialog that asks for a path name to a file. Map requirements are very basic—*Railroad Tycoon II* requires that all imported maps be indexed grayscale images in PCX format. If you are using maps from Cartesia's map collection use the *xxx_ce.pcx* files and convert them to an indexed gray scale *.pcx* image.

> IF YOU WANT TO IMPORT SOME OTHER TYPE OF STARTING IMAGE, THE FILE MUST BE A .PCX FILE WITH AN INDEXED GRAYSCALE PALETTE. ABSOLUTE WHITE WILL SHOW UP AS THE HIGHEST POINTS AND ABSOLUTE BLACK AS THE LOWEST. MAKING THE WATER YOUR LOWEST POINT (BLACK) IN THE IMAGE GIVES THE BEST UNIFORM RESULTS.

5 Next, you'll be shown a slider bar that controls the *smoothness* of the imported image. If you set the number low, very little smoothing will occur; 100 to 150 usually gives you the best results.

6 After you click OK, the image you selected will be turned into a 3D map of the same dimensions as you selected previously. You should try and make the starting image the same general dimensions as the settings, for example, 300 x 300 = a Square = starting image that is a Square. Otherwise your scale and dimensions will be off.

> VERY LARGE MAPS MAY HAVE TO BE MODIFIED HEAVILY DUE TO CURVATURE OF THE EARTH.

7 Once you have an image that is ready to be worked on, save it immediately!

> THE MAP AND SCENARIO DETAILS WILL ALL BE SAVED AT ONE TIME. WHERE YOUR VIEW OF THE MAP IS AT THE TIME OF SAVING AND WHICH LIGHTING ANGLE/ROTATION WILL BE THE VIEW, ANGLE, AND STATUS WHEN THE MAP IS REOPENED. NATURALLY, YOU CAN SAVE OVER THE CURRENT MAP AGAIN.

ROUGHING IN YOUR NEW MAP

If everything went according to plan, you should now have a base map that, while impressive, still has to be transformed into its playing state. The following is the sequence we suggest for use while creating your map, as it seems to be the most dependable.

ADDING LAKES, SEAS, AND OCEANS

Adding lakes, seas, or oceans is a straightforward process. You should do this first to make sure you have set things up correctly—it's tougher to go back and add large bodies of water after everything else is in place. To add water:

1 Select the **Fill Terrain** button (the spilling paint bucket). You will see a display of all of the general terrain tiles used in the game. Along the far right side you'll find the control options for using the fill command:

All—This option modifies all terrain of a particular type.

Adjacent—This option modifies only territory that is adjacent to where you click on the map. With this option selected, you will modify only the nearby terrain of a particular type.

Match—This option acts on all tiles that match the one you click the spilling bucket icon on.

Above—This command affects all the tiles *above* the elevation you click the spilling bucket icon on.

Below—This command affects all the tiles *below* the elevation you click the spilling bucket icon on.

BEFORE YOU DO ANY CLICKING, BE SURE TO HAVE A SAVED VERSION OF YOUR BASE MAP. TUCK THIS AWAY IN A SAFE PLACE BEFORE CONTINUING.

2   Select the water tile...the vibrant blue one on the far right side. Then select *All* and *Below*. Move your spilling bucket icon to the area you've determined is your water (the selection point is the end of the spill), and left-click. As you move the icon around, you should have noticed the areas being highlighted? The highlighted area is where the change will occur.

The water tile is the only tile that will modify the terrain by leveling. Adding the large bodies of water first will give you the quickest feedback as to the general accuracy of your map. It also allows more accurate placement of cities and other features.

ADDING RIVERS

Once the bodies of water are complete, it's time to add the rivers. There is only one river type in *Railroad Tycoon II*, so choosing which one to use is simple. Crossing large bodies of water is impossible, so rivers are your only solution for adding water that can be bridged by players. Here's how you do it:

1   Select the **Build a New Building** button on the bottom right side (the hammer icon). When you click on it, you'll be given a hammer cursor with an arrow tip on the end. The default item selected is the *Lay River* option.

2   Place the icon on the map, then left-click and drag slowly. A river should be forming. You'll likely notice that gaps will start forming. Turn on the Grid (CTRL+G) so that you can see where it needs to be connected.

IF THE GAME SPEED IS SET AT 8 OR HIGHER, IT BECOMES DIFFICULT TO SEE WHICH DIRECTION THE RIVER IS GOING.

3   If you lay a piece of river that you want to delete, select the **Bulldozer** button (third from the bottom left) and then click on the offending watery sprite.

4   To determine the flow of a river, click at it's mouth. The mouth of the river is where you want most rivers to exit. Just watch the animation of the river.

It's most realistic to add slightly greener grass or more plants near rivers, particularly in more arid areas. Also, pay attention to the slope of the river—try not to have it flow up hills! Occasionally, industries on your map will warp your terrain enough to drag a river or body of water out of alignment.

MAKING MOUNTAINS

Your mountains should have been imported with your image. However, if you wish to add, exaggerate, or create them from scratch, here's a quick lesson:

1   Click the **Raise/Lower Ground** button. You will see three large option buttons and five brush sizes. The first option is the raise/lower ground option—make sure this option is selected and use the very first brush..

2   Turn on the Grid (CTRL+G) and place the cursor over your map. You'll see that the cursor highlights the area to be effected.

3   Click and hold the left mouse button and drag the mouse up and down. The terrain will raise and lower as you move the mouse. Once you have positioned it where you want it, release the mouse button.

Since this is your first try, you more than likely made a mess. However, you probably realize how it's done now, so practice to get the look you want.

To turn the high peaks into the mountain tile set, you could start laboriously painting each grid with the mountain tile. Or you can use the Fill Terrain option. To do this:

1   Select the **Fill Terrain** option and select the mountain tile.

2   Choose the options *All* and *Above*, then drag the cursor over the peaks of your mountains. You'll see the affected area highlighted. Click when the highlight suites your design.

Voila! Mountain peaks. Snow works exactly the same, but select the snow terrain tile. This takes a bit of tweaking so don't get discouraged if it looks a little odd, just paint over the areas or reload the map.

You have now learned the basics to create the more obvious geologic features. You should spend some time experimenting. Try new things to see what happens and give yourself a feel for the controls. Changing the brush sizes will give you a variety of results—the best way to find out what they do is to try them. Words will only make the easy seem difficult.

ADDING DETAIL TO YOUR MAPS

With a roughed-in map, you can begin the process of making the details that will make the map playable. This is fun but slow going.

THE TOOLS

You've already played with the Tool controls, but we'll explain each option in a bit more detail. The main tools you'll need for working with maps are located along the edges of the Main Window:

- **Raise/Lower Ground**—This option enables you to raise or lower the ground by left-clicking and dragging grid vertices. The small brush allows more fine detail like

creating valleys, while the large brush should be used to raise plateaus or lower large areas of ground.

- **Smooth Out an Area**—This tool is perhaps your most powerful tool and has two functions. By selecting a brush size then left-clicking and dragging the mouse over an area, the map will "average" the areas highlighted, taking out rough spots. Alternately, if you hold the SHIFT key down and move the cursor over the area you want to change, it will level the area to the center point of the area you first select. This is a forced level and can be very slow on some computers. However, it is a great way to create leveled paths through mountains and water edges. The smallest brush has no effect with this option. Whenever you use this control it is best done with the Grid (CTRL+G). Be aware that smoothing also works on water.

- **Lower an Area to Sea Level**—Depending on the brush size, this can be useful in getting the edges of a body of water to be flat. Use this sparingly—it is best to do this by individual clicks, rather than the click-and-drag method.

- **Paint Brush**—This control enables you to paint the tiles with an appropriate tile type or terrain.

- **Solid**—This option will show you all of the basic tile types. When you paint with these tiles they will replace any tile type they cover, including water.

- **Mix**—This option will show you a grouping of tile *ranges*. These will show the mix and the approximate proportions of each type. When you paint the map with these, they will *not* replace water, snow, or mountain tiles. This is a great way to get that natural feel to the terrain.

SETTING UP TERRITORIES

SETTING UP A TERRITORY IS DONE BY PAINTING ONE ON A MAP, THEN RIGHT-CLICKING ON IT TO SET ITS PROPERTIES:

- **NAME**—THIS IS THE NAME THAT WILL APPEAR IN THE COMPANY BOOKS AND WHEN PLAYERS RIGHT-CLICK ON A TERRITORY. LEFT-CLICK THE TEXT BOX AND TYPE IN THE APPROPRIATE NAME.

- **DEFAULT GOODWILL**—THIS IS IMPORTANT IN DETERMINING THE SPEED OR DIRECTION OF EXPANSION BY THE PLAYER(S). THE RATING YOU GIVE WILL APPLY TO ALL PLAYERS SO YOU MUST THINK GLOBALLY. YOU CAN CHANGE A PARTICULAR PLAYER'S RATING IN A PARTICULAR COUNTRY IN THE EVENT EDITOR. THIS IS YOUR BASE LEVEL SETTING FOR ALL PLAYERS. IF YOU'RE NOT SURE, SET THIS TO 60 OR 65 AS THIS IS A FRIENDLY BUT NOT TOO FRIENDLY RELATION.

- **BORDER IS VISIBLE**—IF THIS IS CHECKED, THE TERRITORY WILL SHOW UP BOTH ON THE MAP AND IN THE COMPANY BOOKS. IT WILL BE ADDRESSABLE THROUGHOUT THE GAME AND HAS DIRECT IMPACT ON THE GAME AT ALL TIMES. IF THIS IS NOT CHECKED, ANOTHER DIALOG WILL POP UP AND PROMPT YOU FOR ADDITIONAL INFORMATION. YOU'LL HAVE TO ASSIGN IT A MIMIC NUMBER OR MAP TO NUMBER. CHECKING

THE RIGHT CLICK MAP BOX WILL FORCE THE TERRITORY TO APPEAR STATISTICALLY LIKE THE MAPPED TO TERRITORY.

- **ALLOW SEPARATE RIGHTS PURCHASE**—IF CHECKED, THIS WILL ALLOW THE PLAYER TO PURCHASE THE RIGHTS TO TRACK LAYING AND TRAIN RUNNING IN THAT TERRITORY SEPARATELY. YOU WILL HAVE TO INPUT THE COST OF SUCH RIGHTS PURCHASING.

- **ACCESS RIGHTS**—HERE YOU SET THE COSTS AND AVAILABILITY OF THE TYPE OF ACCESS RIGHT. IF NO OPTION IS CHECKED, THAT TERRITORY WILL NOT ALLOW THAT ACCESS RIGHT UNLESS YOU HAVE AN EVENT THAT LATER ALLOWS IT DURING THE GAME. YES, THIS CAN GET MESSY, BUT ONCE YOU'VE SET A TERRITORY UP IT GETS VERY CLEAR.

A FEW POINTERS ARE IN ORDER HERE—TERRITORIES ARE VERY USEFUL AS HOTSPOTS FOR EVENTS. IF A CITY OR LOCATION FIGURES VERY HEAVILY IN THE DESIGN OF YOUR MAP, CONSIDER GIVING IT ITS OWN TERRITORY EVEN IF YOU MAKE IT INVISIBLE. THERE CAN ONLY BE 31 TERRITORIES ON A MAP AND THEY CAN NOT BE ERASED FROM THE LIST, ONLY MODIFIED AND OR IGNORED. IN OTHER WORDS, YOU HAVE 31 TERRITORY SLOTS THAT ARE NOT ALWAYS USED BUT ALWAYS AVAILABLE. THE NUMBER YOU SEE IN FRONT OF THE NAME IS THE TERRITORIES ID NUMBER.

- **Add Trees**—This control enables you to add vegetation to your map. This will add trees to the area directly in the highlighted area of the cursor on the map. The more you left-click or move the mouse back and forth while holding down the left mouse button down, the more trees get placed.

- **Cut Down Trees**—This will cull or thin out trees in the area directly in the highlighted area of the cursor on the map. It thins in an opposite manner to the Add Tree brush—the more you move the brush back and forth, the thinner the tree placement becomes.

- **Territories**—Territories enable you to design hot spots as well as generic locations on your maps. This option will allow you to "paint" a territory on your map. Territories are used for geographical reference and for supporting scenario events. Automatically, you will always begin with one territory. Any new territories need to be added and set up in order to function and be available in the event editor. (For more details on Territories, see the sidebar, "Setting—Up Territories.")

- **Build a New Building**.—This control contains options for placing all the objects on to the map world that are not directly controlled by stations. These include industries, regions, labels, cities, reserve cells, and rivers.

- **Industries**—This option enables you to place industries in locations that will never change. They can still go out of business during gameplay; however they always appear in the same place at the start of a game. If you place these in a scenario in which you have already created a company, they will be owned by the player. To correct this, don't build a company first, or sell them once they've been built.

- **Regions**.—This allows you to place a marker for a resource area. Once you put a marker down, you can set the resource levels by left-clicking on the region icon. You will be given a list of all the industries in the game that have not been restricted in the editor. Each industry will be given a slider to adjust the

likelihood of that industry appearing in that region. (For more details on Regions, see the sidebar, "Regions at a Glance.")

- **Labels**—These are simple tags that you can insert into the map that do not effect the gameplay. They will appear as white lettered labels during play.
- **Cities**—Here you have several settings that must be addressed in order to create a city:

  City: Left-click in this dialog box and type in the name of the city you wish to create.

  Size: This will determine the number of buildings in this population center. Table 9-1 lists the various possible sizes.

  Architecture: Choose the default style of station that will be built in the area of this population center.

REGIONS AT A GLANCE

REGIONS ALWAYS EXPAND TO BORDER EACH OTHER. IF YOU PLACE ONE REGION, IT WILL EXPAND TO THE ENTIRE MAP. TWO REGIONS WILL DIVIDE THE MAP RELATIVE TO THEIR LOCATION TO THE EDGE AND THE CENTER OF THE OTHER REGION. REGIONS CAN HAVE ZERO OR MORE INDUSTRIES IN IT BASED ON THE PERCENT CHANCE OF IT APPEARING IN THAT AREA.

FOR EXAMPLE, REGION A HAS MILK = 20 PERCENT AND COAL = 12 PERCENT. EVERY TIME AN INDUSTRY IS GROWN IN THIS REGION IT WILL BE OF ONE OF THESE INDUSTRIES. IN THIS CASE IT IS SLIGHTLY MORE LIKELY TO BE MILK.

RAISING BOTH NUMBERS HIGHER TENDS TO INCREASE THE NUMBER OF THE INDUSTRIES IN THE REGION BUT NOT THE RATIO. FINALLY, BUILDING DENSITY CAN BE SET. THE HIGHER THE DENSITY THE MORE INDUSTRIES (HIGH TENDS TO BE TOO MUCH AND LOW TO LITTLE, SO YOU'LL NEED TO EXPERIMENT). YOU CAN ALSO EXPERIMENT WITH BUILDING NULL REGIONS TO SPREAD OUT INDUSTRIES AS NECESSARY. ALL OTHER OPTIONS DISPLAYED ARE SELF-EXPLANATORY.

QUICK TIP: IT'S BETTER TO PUT THE RAW MATERIAL INDUSTRIES IN THE COUNTRYSIDE AND THE MANUFACTURERS IN THE CITIES. IF IN DOUBT, LEAVE SETTINGS ON 25 PERCENT OR LESS.

TABLE 9-1. CITY SIZES

SIZE	APPEARANCE
Village	1 to 2 buildings are likely; if an industry is set for this population center, few houses will show up with it, if any.
Town	1 to 4 buildings are likely; usually no more that 2 houses are likely to appear if an industry is set for this population center.
City	4 to 8 buildings are likely; any combination of industries and housing will appear.
Metropolis	6 to 11 buildings are likely; any combination of industries and housing will appear.
Megopolis	8+ buildings are likely; any combination of industries and housing will appear.

SETTING UP A PLAYER OR AI COMPANY

To set up a player or AI company, you must first select the player you wish to assign to this company in the Player List Box:

1. To select the player, click *Switch Control To The Next Player* (at the very bottom of the Player List Box) to cycle through the players you set up in the *Game Options*.

2. Once your player is selected, you have to switch the Center List Box to the Company List Box. In the Center List Box, double-click the Start Company option. This will bring up the normal Start Company dialog. Select the settings as you desire and click *OK*.

If you wish to build buildings for this company—AI or human—just start building the way you normally would during the game.

To adjust company cash, double-click the company you wish to modify in the Company List Box. This should display the first page of the company books under *Overview*. On the right-hand page, you'll see three options:

- **Liquidate Company**—This option will clear the company from the game; however, if the company had any assets placed on the map, they will remain as non-owned structures.

- **Set Cash**—This selection will give you the option of typing in the amount of money you wish the company to have.

- **Change Company Name/Logo**—Click here to bring up the dialog that enables you to change your company name and logo.

To adjust a player's cash, double-click on the player in the Player List Box. This will show you the player name and description. Also you'll have the option to set the amount of starting money the player has. You can then enter the stock market to buy up or sell additional stocks.

When placing the infrastructure for AI companies on the map, be sure that the AI has all train and track rights to the territory (or territories) in which they exist.

Never give the AI too much *personal* starting cash. The AI is very efficient in buying up player stocks and such. This can potentially make the game too lopsided and no fun.

AI COMPANIES CHAIRED BY A STOCK-MANIPULATING CHARACTER WILL TEND TO GO OUT OF BUSINESS QUICKLY UNLESS THE ROUTE IS EASY MONEY. CHECK THE CHAIRMEN CHART BEFORE PLACING ONE IN A PIVOTAL COMPANY ROLE.

GENERAL MAP-MAKING TIPS

To wrap things up, here are a few general tips to help you as you begin making maps. These are by no means exhaustive, but they will give you information that you should be able to put to use immediately:

- To create level corridors or valleys, use the Smooth tool with the SHIFT key option. Click and advance your cursor in small increments. This is great for grading riverbeds and valleys. The smallest of the brushes does not work for this tool.

- Use the Grid (CTRL+G). It will save you countless little mistakes and show you the true lay of the land.

- Turn off the tree graphics when working on the map except when you are placing the trees. Things will get too cluttered otherwise.

- Use the largest appropriate brush when placing your trees. Go in and thin out the trees—with the chain saw if necessary. This tends to produce more natural looking results.

- Exaggerate the size of mountains a little. They tend to get lost in the grand scheme of things and are often less inspiring than other features.

- Place your cities along the coastline and waterways first. These cities tend to be easier to accurately locate and can later be used to triangulate the location of cities with few or no identifiable geographic markers.

- Use the Smooth tool with the SHIFT key option to level any uneven water. The sea level tool may not be the right one for many of your inland bodies of water.

- Try to avoid grades of above 8 percent on known routes unless it is the desired effect.

- Try to keep city centers 17 or more squares from each other for the best play performance.

- Rotate the map occasionally as you build. This will help you catch surface deformations and anomalies.

Experiment. Nothing can replace the insight and feel for map-making. You can best hone your skill through trial and a little error.

The Event Editor

THE RAILROAD TYCOON II EVENT EDITOR IS A
MAJOR COMPONENT OF THE INTEGRATED
EDITOR IN THE GAME. EVENTS ARE BASICALLY
THE WILDCARD THAT YOU CAN USE TO DO JUST
ABOUT ANYTHING THAT ISN'T A REGULAR PART
OF THE GAMEPLAY. EVENTS ENABLE YOU
TO INTRODUCE UNIQUE CIRCUMSTANCES
INTO SCENARIOS, SUCH AS THE HEAVY
GOVERNMENT BONUSES FOR THE AMERICAN
TRANSCONTINENTAL RAILROADS, THE
EUROPEAN PUSH FOR ELECTRIFICATION, THE
EXCLUSIVE TRACK-BUILDING LICENSES ISSUED
BY UNPREDICTABLE SOUTH AMERICAN
GOVERNMENTS, AND MORE. AN EVENT IS ONE
SET OF EFFECTS THAT RESULTS FROM ONE
TRIGGER CONDITION. BY CREATING ONE OR
MORE EVENTS, YOU CHANGE THE RULES OF
THE GAME AND CREATE A SCENARIO THAT IS
UNIQUE NOT ONLY IN GEOGRAPHY, BUT ALSO
IN HISTORICAL FLAVOR AND CONDITIONS.

WORKING WITH THE EVENT EDITOR

The event editor is accessed through the **map options** window in the **map editor**. Click on the events item in the list at the left, and you'll see a list box with all current events in it. Most likely there won't be any if you're working on a map you've just created. To add a new event, click the Add button. The event editor window will now be in place. There are four basic elements to an event:

- **Trigger** determines what causes the event and what does it affect
- **Message Text** determines what message, if any, is displayed to the player when this event occurs
- **Frequency** determines how often the game checks for this event's occurrence
- **Effect** determines what, if any, gameplay changes occur when this event happens

YOU CAN ALSO ADD NOTES ON THE EVENT IN THE COMMENTS BOX. COMMENTS ARE FOR QUICK REFERENCE TO THE EVENT AND ARE DISPLAYED IN THE EVENTS LIST BOX. THEY HAVE NO IMPACT OTHER THAN TO HELP DOCUMENT THE EVENT. IF A COMMENT IS ENTERED, IT APPEARS ON THE LIST OF EVENTS IN THE MAP OPTIONS WINDOW, WHICH CAN BE HELPFUL TO KEEP TRACK OF THE PURPOSE OF THE INDIVIDUAL EVENTS. IT IS BEST TO PLACE SPECIFIC INFORMATION AS IT RELATES TO THE CAMPAIGN AT HAND.

To edit an existing event you can either double-click the event you wish to edit or highlight it and then click the edit button at the bottom of the list box.

FOR A DETAILED LIST OF ALL TRIGGERED EVENTS, SEE APPENDIX C: FUNCTIONS AND EFFECTS.

TRIGGERS

Triggers determine if the event occurs, and to whom the event occurs (if applicable). Triggers are the equivalent of *"if"* statements in programming, and actually work pretty much the same. A simple trigger would be something like the following:

```
GameYear = 1875
```

This trigger will evaluate to false for any year in the game except 1875. If the trigger evaluates to false, the event will not occur, and none of the effects or text will happen. The event will

normally be re-evaluated later, depending on the Frequency setting, and may evaluate to true at a later time.

A trigger is made up of one or more individual elements, which the computer will evaluate to resolve the overall statement as true or false. However, sometimes you want to evaluate the trigger multiple times, against multiple companies, players, or territories. That's what the checkboxes on this panel are for. If the Test Against Multiple Companies check box is on, then the trigger will be evaluated against each company, and if it is true one or more times, then the events and text will occur one or more times, to the individual companies in question. For example, if you wanted to levy a special government tax against any company that was overly profitable, you might create the following trigger:

```
CompanyNetIncomeThisYear > 1000000
```

Assume the effect is that $50,000 is taken away from the company. If there are four companies in the game when this event is evaluated, with earnings of $100,000, $1,200,000, -$20,000, and $2,000,000 respectively, then the trigger would evaluate to false for the first and the third company, and true for the second and fourth, with the effect ($50,000 penalty each) being taken from both the second and the fourth company.

> FOR COMPANIES AND PLAYERS, YOU HAVE THE ABILITY TO FURTHER LIMIT THINGS BY ONLY TESTING AGAINST HUMAN- OR COMPUTER-CONTROLLED COMPANIES OR PLAYERS. A COMPANY IS CONSIDERED HUMAN CONTROLLED IF ITS CHAIRMAN IS A HUMAN PLAYER, COMPUTER CONTROLLED IF ITS CHAIRMAN IS A COMPUTER PLAYER, OR IF IT HAS NO CHAIRMAN.

You can also choose to limit a trigger by making it a one-time-only event. If this is checked, the event will be evaluated as per a normal event, at normal frequencies, but after the first time it has evaluated to true (regardless of how many previous times it has evaluated to false), it is disabled and not checked again. If an event is being evaluated against multiple players, companies, or territories, it will *not* continue on down the list, it will stop after the first true evaluation against a player, company, or territory.

The evaluation order for players, companies, and territories is the same as the order they appear in their various list boxes, top to bottom. Events themselves are evaluated in the order they appear in the event list box on the map options window.

Expressions are constructed out of the multiple types of elements, as illustrated in the following complex trigger:

```
GameYear >= 1872 AND (CompanyGoodwill>10 OR
    CompanyCash(IsHighestInClass) OR
    CompanyDebt * 3 < CompanyTotalAssets)
```

TRIGGER ELEMENTS

The following elements are used in this trigger:

- **Numeric constants**—The numbers 1872, 10, and 3 are numeric constants. Constants must be integers (no decimals). Don't use comma separators for thousands (23,400). Also, don't use dollar signs or anything else other than the raw digits between "0" and "9", and the "+" or "-" sign (-3).

- **Comparators**—To compare two subexpressions, the following comparators may be used:

>=	greater than or equal to
<=	less than or equal to
>	greater than
<	less than
=	equal to
!=	not equal to (the opposite of equal to)
AND	is equal to true if both the left half and the right half of an expression are true
OR	is equal to true if either the left half or the right half of an expression are true

- **Expression joiners**—These are used to combine two values using ordinary arithmetic. Expression joiners include

+	Add the left and right side
-	Subtract the right side from the left side
*	Multiply the left and the right side
/	Divide the left side by the right side, if right side is 0, always evaluates to 1

- **Parentheses ( )**—Parentheses serve a dual function. When immediately following a function name, they serve to enclose the parameter for the function (for example, `CompanyCash(IsHighestInClass)` where `IsHighestInClass` is a parameter). In all other instances, parentheses are used to control the order in which expressions are evaluated, with the innermost expressions evaluated first. This can be very important, as in the following expression:

  3 * 2 + 2 = 8   evaluates to true (The left side evaluates to 8)

  3 * (2 + 2) = 8 evaluates to false (The left side evaluates to 12)

- **Functions**—Functions are certain keywords that the game knows how to evaluate, such as `CompanyCash`, `GameYear`, and `PlayerNetWorth`. Many functions also have an optional or mandatory parameter, which is enclosed in parenthesis immediately after the function name. For example, `CompanyCash(IsHighestInClass)` will only evaluate to true if the company in question has the most cash of everything in its class (other companies), that is, it finds the wealthiest company. Some parameters are words (`IsHighestInClass`, `IsLowestInClass`), and some are numbers (3). A full list of functions and their correct usage is included in Appendix C, Functions and Effects.

EVALUATION ORDER

Expressions are evaluated by type of element first, then from left to right within type. You can always use parentheses to override the default evaluation order if you so desire. The order of type evaluation is:

1 **Functions**—Functions and their parameters are evaluated to produce numeric results; for example, `CompanyCash(IsHighestInClass)` is reduced to true or false

2 **Parentheses**—Expressions within parentheses are evaluated following this order, innermost enclosed expressions first:

> multiply (*) and divide (/) operations are performed
>
> plus (+) and minus (-) operations are performed
>
> Expression joiners (< > <= >= =) reduce expressions on the left and right side to either true or false
>
> The remaining values are combined using AND and OR

A WORD ON FUNCTIONS

There are over 70 functions available to you in the event editor, allowing you a lot of freedom to create just about any kind of trigger you can imagine.

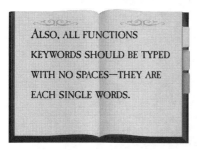

> ALSO, ALL FUNCTIONS KEYWORDS SHOULD BE TYPED WITH NO SPACES—THEY ARE EACH SINGLE WORDS.

Some functions require an ID as a parameter. An ID is a numeric value that is associated with a particular company, player, territory, or city. Proper syntax is as follows:

```
TerritoryConnectedToTerritory(4)
```

Some functions take an optional class parameter. There are two class parameters: `IsHighestInClass` and `IsLowestInClass`. They return true if the value returned by that function is higher (or lower) than that returned by anything else in the same class (such as other companies, in the case of CompanyCash). For `CompanyTerritory` functions, the comparison will be against other companies given the current territory, not vice versa. The proper syntax is as follows:

```
CompanyCash(IsHighestInClass)
```

OTHER TRIGGER SETTINGS

Here's a list of other available Trigger settings:

- **One Time Only Event**—This check box determines if this event can only occur once in the game. If the box is checked it means it should be a one-time event. Combinations of these can occur.
- **Test Against Multiple Companies**—Test the trigger against every active company in the game independently. This can be further limited to only checking against computer-controlled or human-controlled companies by checking one of the other check boxes listed.
- **Test Against Multiple Players**—Test the trigger against every active player in the game independently. This can be further limited to only checking against computer or human companies by checking one of the other check boxes listed.
- **Test Against Territories**—This trigger tests against the territories in the game. This is another way of limiting the calculation of the event. For example, the result may be "If Territory X is not friendly to player by 1880, then player loses".

> EVENTS ARE EVALUATED FROM THE TOP OF THE LIST DOWN. THIS IS PARTICULARLY IMPORTANT IN SEQUENCING OF END-OF-YEAR/MONTH AND END-OF-GAME EVENTS. IF THE EVENT IS CHECKED EQUALLY FOR AN "END OF" EVENT THEN THE FIRST ONE LISTED IS EVALUATED BEFORE THE NEXT ONE. THEREFORE IT COULD END AN EVENT OR THE SCENARIO BEFORE IT GOT TO THE NEXT EVENT. PLACE YOUR EVENTS CAREFULLY.

MESSAGE TEXT

This is where you deliver your information to the players. Left-clicking anywhere in that box will enable you to begin typing. The HOME key will take you to the beginning of the text and the END key will take you to the end of the text. This is the only way for you to pass along necessary information or develop a story line.

AN EVENT DOESN'T HAVE TO HAVE ANY TEXT AT ALL. IF YOU DO NOT PUT IN ANY TEXT HERE, THE EVENT WILL BE SILENT AND NOT SHOW UP IN THE GAME AS A VIEWABLE EVENT. INSTEAD IT WILL TAKE PLACE WHEN TRIGGERED BUT NOT NOTIFY THE PLAYER. SNEAKY. HOWEVER, IF YOU DO ENTER ANYTHING IN THE TEXT SECTION, THEN THE GAME WILL SHOW THAT PIECE OF TEXT WHEN THE EVENT OCCURS, UNLESS THE EVENT ONLY AFFECTS ANOTHER PLAYER OR A COMPANY YOU DON'T CONTROL, IN WHICH CASE THE TEXT WILL NOT SHOW.

You can choose one of three formats for the text to appear in: Dialog, Newspaper, and Choice. To begin your message input first select one of the top three radio buttons in the Message Dialog:

- **Dialog**—Selecting this option will give you the simplest method of messaging. Any text you enter into the text box will be displayed to the player in a simple dialog box with an OK button to clear.

THE DIALOG WINDOW IS USED FOR LONGER MESSAGES. IT'S THE WINDOW WITH THE EAGLE AT THE TOP AND THE ENGINE FRONT END AT THE BOTTOM.

- **Newspaper**—Here you will have two text boxes to fill out. The first is titled HEADLINE. Information text in this box will appear in large type at the top of the newspaper dialog. Remember, keep this text as short and dynamic as possible as it is the HEADLINE of a newspaper and not a simple description or a chalkboard. The second text box is titled SUB HEADLINE. This is a sub-heading where newspapers customarily enter a smaller more detailed description of the headline story. We follow the same concept here. Care should be taken when writing these sub-descriptions, as there is a finite amount of space that the message can display before being cut off. This amount is variable, depending on the letters used, as their spacing can affect how the message is shown on-screen. It's always a good idea to test events using the newspaper option to see if the text you want to display is shut off.

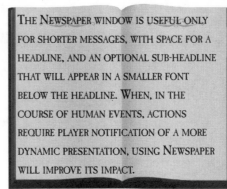

THE NEWSPAPER WINDOW IS USEFUL ONLY FOR SHORTER MESSAGES, WITH SPACE FOR A HEADLINE, AND AN OPTIONAL SUB-HEADLINE THAT WILL APPEAR IN A SMALLER FONT BELOW THE HEADLINE. WHEN, IN THE COURSE OF HUMAN EVENTS, ACTIONS REQUIRE PLAYER NOTIFICATION OF A MORE DYNAMIC PRESENTATION, USING NEWSPAPER WILL IMPROVE ITS IMPACT.

- **Choice**—The Choice dialog allows you to collect player input and create a more dynamic and personalized experience. First you'll have a text box that functions as a normal dialog; however it must be used to set up the two smaller sub-boxes, Button 1 Label and Button 2 Label. These buttons will be displayed to the player as the two obvious choices. Selecting one of the buttons will trigger the event you've set up for that particular button. You can create these button effects by selecting that button's event listed on the left side. It's important to remember that this is the only way for you to receive data from your players and provide them with a measure of control over events.

THE CHOICE WINDOW IS ACTUALLY AN INTERESTING VARIANT ON THE DIALOG WINDOW, USING THAT EAGLE WINDOW TO DISPLAY TEXT. HOWEVER, INSTEAD OF HAVING A SIMPLE OK BUTTON AT THE BOTTOM TO CONFIRM THE MESSAGE, YOU GET TO PUT TWO BUTTONS, LABELED AS YOU CHOOSE, WITH THE USER'S CHOICE RESULTING IN DIFFERENT EFFECTS. THE CHOICE WINDOW IS USEFUL FOR SUCH SITUATIONS AS OFFERING THE PLAYER THE CHANCE TO BUY RIGHTS TO AN ENGINE FOR A CERTAIN AMOUNT OF MONEY. FOR EXAMPLE, THE "YES" CHOICE COULD HAVE AN EFFECT OF PROVIDING THE ENGINE RIGHTS AND SUBTRACTING THE CASH. THE "NO" CHOICE COULD HAVE NO EFFECT, OR SOME ALTOGETHER DIFFERENT EFFECT. NOTE THAT WHEN CHOICE TEXT IS SELECTED, THERE ARE TWO DIFFERENT EFFECT ITEMS ON THE LIST AT THE LEFT, ONE FOR EACH ALTERNATIVE CHOICE. HERE IS A MORE DYNAMIC PLAYER INTERFACE.

FREQUENCY

The Frequency settings enable you to determine when your events will be checked. Each mode is self-explanatory. Checking every time a track or station is placed is usually used in conjunction with a territory.

Evaluating complex events takes CPU time, and can slow down the game, particularly if there are a lot of them. So you can choose to evaluate events only yearly, or go for the more frequent monthly checks if you choose. Note that for each you can choose the end of the period, or the beginning of the following period. This can be an important distinction, because the date will have changed, possibly effecting some date-based triggers, and at the beginning of the year, the year-to-date numbers for many variables are reset to zero (0).

There is one other alternative here—to evaluate the event every time track or stations are placed down or removed (by either human or computer players). This is particularly useful for events relating to places being connected by track to other places, which would only occur upon new track and station placement.

EFFECTS

Effects are the gameplay changes that occur in response to triggers. Triggers are the target and conditions that must be met before an effect takes place.

There are some 250+ effects in the game (see Appendix C, Functions and Effects). Each effect has a range or value that can be adjusted by the slider bar immediately to the right of its listing in the event editor under effects. Adjusting the slider bar will display the value directly under the bar itself. Additionally, a tally of the number of effects modified for that event is maintained at the bottom of the effects list box. If you leave and then return to the effects of an event, you'll find the modified effects listed at the top of the list box.

Any event can be composed of any or all of the 250+ effects; however some combinations may be contradictory and invalidate each other. We recommend writing out your events *before* you enter them as means of tracking any problems that may occur before or after implementing the event.

Effects can be divided into three general categories:

- **Performance**—These effects govern the greatest variety of play modifiers and have the ability to alter play at the most exacting level. This group also includes the Game Over triggers, which naturally can stop a game cold. These effects tend to have the most dynamic affects on the scenario.

- **Cargo and Items**—These effects govern all of the cargo values and production rates. When adjusting these, keep in mind the scale of the game, since an increase of production by just 1 can *double* the output of many resources.

- **Variables**—These effects function more as tools for you to create more complex events. There are four categories of variables:

    Global variables, which affect the entire game

    Company variables, which affect only a specific company or companies.

    Player variables, which effect the player/chairman.

    Territories variables, which affect activities within a specific territory or territories.

There are four definable variables for each category numbered 1 through 4 in two distinct classifications, Add To and Set. *Add To* works as a counter allowing the use of positive and negative numbers. *Set* works as a defined level or setting. For example, Global variables all have a range of -99 to 100 and are considered *instant* (see **Instant** below).

Above the events list box you will see the *duration* modifier and immediately to its right you will see two radio buttons: Permanent and Temporary. *Permanent* means that this (these) effect(s) will stay in effect until another effect changes them. *Temporary* means this (these) effect(s) have a limited duration. If this is selected you will be prompted for the number of **years** and **months** that you wish these effects to be in effect. You may respond in months and the program will automatically divide them into years and months.

> TEMPORARY WILL NOT MODIFY THOSE EFFECTS LISTED AS INSTANT. (FOR MORE DETAILS SEE INSTANT BELOW.)

An effect that is listed as an **instant** effect indicates that it can not be turned off by the program by making the entire event *temporary.* Therefore all instant effects are persistent, should you wish to turn off this effect you must create another event that performs this task, for example

```
trigger = GameYear>=1880, effect = Territory Confiscate All.
    To change: trigger = (can be any legal trigger)
    GameYear>=1885, effect = Territory Confiscate None.
```

The desired effect was to confiscate any items that were in or being built in the specified territory from 1880 until 1885. Remember that an event can be silent if you don't enter any message text.

IMPORTANT HINTS FOR USING EVENTS AND TRIGGERS

HERE ARE SOME THINGS TO KEEP IN MIND WHEN WORKING WITH EVENTS AND TRIGGERS:

- REMEMBER THAT THE TRIGGERS ARE EVALUATED FROM THE TOP DOWN.
- THE AI DOES NOT KNOW HOW TO BUY INTO TERRITORIES. IF YOU WISH THE AI TO HAVE ACCESS TO SOME, NONE, OR ALL, YOU WILL HAVE TO TELL IT WHICH ONES. TO HAVE IT CHECK ALL TERRITORIES FOR AN ON OR OFF EVENT, DO NOT INCLUDE A TERRITORY ID NUMBER IN THE TRIGGER AND JUST CHECK THE TEST AGAINST TERRITORIES BOX.
- TRY AND SIMPLIFY WHAT GETS CHECKED FOR AN EVENT TO KEEP FROM HAVING BURIED MISTAKES. USE THE TEST AGAINST CHECK BOX WHEN POSSIBLE INSTEAD OF ID NUMBERS.
- LISTING YOUR VICTORY CONDITIONS FROM GOLD THROUGH TO LOSE TENDS TO AVOID SEQUENCING ERRORS (TRUST US).
- MOST ERRORS COME FROM AN INCORRECTLY SELECTED FREQUENCY CHOICE. CHECK THEM WHEN IN DOUBT.
- MISUSE OF THE < > SIGNS IS ANOTHER PROBLEM. BE SURE YOU'RE EVALUATING THEM THE WAY YOU NEED TO.
- SINCE MOST GENERAL TRIGGERS ARE EITHER AT THE BEGINNING OR END OF THE MONTH, MOST EVENTS HAPPEN THEN. TO BREAK THAT CONGESTION UP, ADD OR CHANGE DATED EVENTS TO A GAMEYEARMONTH TRIGGER IF POSSIBLE.
- TO CREATE A "SILENT" EVENT, JUST DO NOT ADD ANY TEXT. THIS WILL NOT TRIGGER A DIALOG BOX OR NEWSPAPER.
- GAMES SET IN THE YEARS AFTER 1950 CAN BECOME A BIT TOUGH FINANCIALLY. YOU MAY NEED TO GLOBALLY CHANGE THE PRODUCTION RATE FOR INDUSTRIES AND OR REVENUES FOR THEM. THIS IS NOT GENERALLY THE CASE BUT COMPLEX SCENARIOS OFTEN CAUSE THE TIGHT PROFIT MARGINS SIMULATED IN LATER YEARS TO BE MORE EXAGGERATED.
- TERRITORIES THAT ARE NOT VISIBLE DO NOT SHOW UP IN THE TERRITORY PAGE OF THE COMPANY BOOKS. THEREFORE, EFFECTS THAT HAPPEN TO THE TERRITORY THEY ARE MAPPED TO HAPPEN TO THE INVISIBLE TERRITORY EQUALLY; FOR EXAMPLE, BUYING INTO THE VISIBLE TERRITORY WILL ALSO BUY INTO THE INVISIBLE ONE.

OTHER EVENT AND MAP SETTINGS

Each setting listed below appears on the event dialog and needs to be addressed before you can create a final map. They tend to be less difficult to grasp than Events and Triggers; however they do have substantial impact and can kill a scenario design if not used properly. Our original intent was to make this game playable by 32 players simultaneously. While it can in theory be played this way, our largest maps (500 x 500) turned out to be functionally too small for each player to have the same type of enjoyment. The magic number on a 500 x 500 map tends to be about 16 to18 This gives each player the possibility of finding some undeveloped space on the map to build, assuming that the map is at least 80 percent or more land. Please keep this in mind, as well as the following:

- **Player**—The following settings determine initial player start options for the map:

  The Allow player to override check box enables the player to use a different chairman in a multiplayer game.

  Unassigned players portraits will be randomly assigned at the start of a game.

  In order to start a company, player cash should be about $100,000. It can be done with less and is an interesting way to start players as investors only.

- **Player Pool**—Here's where you decide which chairmen will be used in your scenario. The three global selections will give you quick filtering of your chairman as a general selection. It tends to be best if you hand pick the available opponents.

- **Managers**—This enables you to include or exclude particular managers from your scenario. We tend to leave everyone in as the larger selection allows for better variables within your game.

- **Economy**—This determines how fast and how profitable the environment is in your scenario. The starting economic level will determine how big your cities will be at the beginning of your game. The annual growth rate is simply how much they grow each year.

- **Engines**—Here you choose which locomotives will be allowed in your scenario. The global filters are more for game play than historical accuracy. Use them only to "thin" out the available engines. An engine not selected here *can* be activated in the game with an event.

- **Industry**—As each industry is highlighted in the list box, the check box next to the picture will have an X if it is to be used in the game. Any industry not checked will not show up in the map even if it is selected in a city or region industry setting.

- **General Restrictions**—This is for the most part self-explanatory. However, it's important to note just how powerful these choices are. They are akin to creating rule sets that can drastically alter the way the game is played. Changes here can make normal strategies vary considerably. Also, the last option—*Player can start multiple companies*—is a bit confusing: What it really means is that they can start *one* (1) company but no others. This is useful in allowing a game where you do not wish a player to start a company after they have lost their first without having to set up their starting company. Setting up a company for the player is required if you use the *Starting a company* restriction.

> ALL OPTIONS HERE SHOULD BE SEEN AS SET TO YES, UNLESS YOU'VE CHECKED THE BOX, FOR EXAMPLE, IF STARTING A COMPANY WERE CHECKED, IT WOULD NOT ALLOW A PLAYER TO START A COMPANY. (YOU MAY WANT THEM TO HAVE TO BUY INTO EXISTING ONES).

- **Special restrictions**— these restrictions allow for unique rules variations that don't fall within normal game parameters. These allowed the creation of the "Whistle Stops and Promises" campaign scenario. They are explained in the hover text on the bottom of

> WHEN BUILDING A SCENARIO WITH THESE OPTIONS, BE SURE TO LEAVE THE GENERAL RESTRICTIONS OFF TILL YOU'VE FINISHED ALL THE MAP MODIFICATIONS YOU WISH TO DO, AS THEY CAN STOP CERTAIN CONSTRUCTION FEATURES TOO.

each option. Slow date makes the game go by in days and hours, where days are years and hours are months. It makes for an entirely different scale and feel for the game. All other features remain the same but now industries produce *daily* instead of *annually*. Cool, huh? Remember that you can use any one of these options separately or in combination with any other game parameter.

- **Ports**—This is how you determine what will be "produced" and "demanded" by the ports in your scenarios. There are four (4) general industrial areas of modification possible in your port settings, not all have to be used. All port settings are global for your map. One port will be the same as any other on your map. Also, ports are the main way of introducing materials into a country that would not normally be able to produce them themselves. Ports function just like industries in terms of buying and profit. The Ports have two special attributes that must be set in order for them to function:

  Annual Supply, which shows what will be produced and the quantity that will be made each year.

  Manufactured Supply, which will be used to either create a simple demand that you select or it will create an exchange. If you also select an Annual

Supply, the two cargoes displayed will be interchanged for each other. For example, the combination `Annual Supply = Steel + Manufactured Supply = iron` would provide one steel for each iron delivered to it.

Ports have the potential to upset your map's industry balance, and it is best to set them once your whole map structure is finalized.

- **Robbers**—You can put the names or titles of the robbers you wish to have in your scenario. Also you can set the frequency and starting year for the robbers. If your named robbers are all captured, then a generic "robber" will be listed.

- **Regional**—These settings effect the global type of map you intend on creating. These global settings are used to represent the location's general railway and populace behaviors. These factors will raise or lower costs for operating engine types described and increase or decrease passenger production.

- **General/Map Setup**— This information shows up in the main map setup screen. It will automatically display the map's dimension in the main setup screen:

  Minimum Start Year is the earliest you intended the game to be begun. If a player attempts to adjust the start year in the main setup page, it will not go lower than this.

  Default Start Year is the year you've decided best suits the scenario for starting.

  Maximum Start Year is the latest you intended the game to be played to be started. If a player attempts to adjust the start year in the main setup page, it will not go higher than this.

  Campaign Map is checked if it is a part of a campaign. There is currently no campaign creation option for users.

> AT THE TIME OF WRITING THIS BOOK, POPTOP HAD PLANS OF MAKING AVAILABLE AN FAQ FOR THE EDITOR THAT SHIPS WITH THE GAME. PLEASE CHECK WWW.POPTOP.COM FOR MORE INFORMATION.

PART VI

MEET THE REAL TYCOONS

EVER WONDERED WHAT THE GAME DESIGNERS, PROGRAMMERS, AND ARTISTS EAT DURING CRUNCH TIME? WHAT GAMES THEY PLAY AFTER HOURS? WHAT STRATEGIES THEY USE TO POUND EACH OTHER IN MULTIPLAYER MODE? TURN THE PAGES AND GET THE SCOOP FROM THE MOST EXPERIENCED RAILROAD TYCOON II PLAYERS—FOR THE TIME BEING, THAT IS.

11

Robber Baron Extraordinaire

AN INTERVIEW WITH PHIL STEINMEYER

IN AN AGE OF LARGE FACELESS PUBLISHERS AND TWELVE-PERSON DESIGN TEAMS, RAILROAD TYCOON II'S DEVELOPMENT WENT AGAINST THE GRAIN. POPTOP SOFTWARE IS A SIX-PERSON COMPANY LOCATED IN THE GAME DEVELOPMENT NETHERWORLD OF ST. LOUIS, MISSOURI. POPTOP IS HEADED BY DESIGNER/PROGRAMMER/PRODUCER PHIL STEINMEYER. IN THIS INTERVIEW PHIL STEINMEYER TALKS ABOUT THE GENESIS OF RAILROAD TYCOON II, THE GAME'S AI, AND THE FUTURE OF GAMING.

How did you get started in the computer game industry?

In early 1993, I decided to teach myself the programming language C, in preparation for a return to computer consulting. I needed a decent sized project to work on, to motivate myself to learn it, and started creating a variation of the old "snake" game (where your snake runs around the screen eating apples and growing longer). After three days of that, I decided to shoot for something more ambitious, going for a computer version of my favorite board game—Squad Leader. I kept working on the project, although after three months, I took a full-time job consulting at the Chicago and Northwestern Railroad. In September 1994, the game, now called Iron Cross, was completed and released. It wasn't a monster hit, but it was successful enough to enable me to quit the consulting job and get into the game biz full-time.

Is there a certain type of game that you would like PopTop to specialize in?

I love strategy games—they're 70 percent of what I've played for the last decade. I like RPGs, too, which I consider pseudo-strategy games. Action games are fun for multi-player (Quake II is a hit around the office), but I don't play them single-player.

That said, PopTop will always focus on strategy games—you have to do what you love.

The original Railroad Tycoon *is a classic by anyone's measure. Designed by gaming legend Sid Meier, it still has a cult following. What made you decide to take on this legendary title? And what was the greatest challenge once you decided walking in the footsteps of an established strategy master?*

I was a huge fan of the original, along with Sid's other classic, *Civilization.* But while Civilization has seen both official and unofficial sequels, no one had done a really top notch railroad game since the release of *Railroad Tycoon* in 1990. I wanted to make the game because I wanted to play the game, and I also thought a lot of other people would want to play it, too.

Definitely the greatest challenge with a sequel like this is meeting the extraordinary expectations for the product. The original is one of the two or three greatest strategy games of all time. You can't make a sequel that's average, or even good. It has to be great or you're going to disappoint a lot of people. However, with all the advances in graphics and gameplay in the last decade, the game clearly had to go way beyond the original. The challenge was adding new stuff without over-complicating the game or destroying the magic of the original.

Railroad Tycoon II *was almost two years in the making. What took the most time in the design process?*

Getting the 3D outside engine up and going took about four to five months. Getting all the other interface screens (train, station, stock, and so on) in took about seven months. The game was basically functional after a year or so, but we spent pretty much all of 1998 tweaking the game, adding stuff to make it more playable and deeper, and to accommodate the wide range of interests people have within railroad noir. This last stage—creating the "magic" of the game, definitely took the longest and was the most challenging.

Railroad Tycoon II *is full of historical detail. How long did it take you to do the research for the game, and what challenges did you run into?*

Fortunately, several of us were pretty familiar with railroads going in. However, the nitty gritty research (which tycoons do we include, what stats do we use for the included engines, and so on)

MEET THE REAL TYCOONS

was done by Franz Felsl, and probably took about three man-months of work.

One challenge was finding pictures of all the tycoons we wanted to include—we ended up faking one of them (you guess which) but overall we found most of what we needed. We also struggled a bit to find models and/or pictures of the engines we wanted. The model railroad industry is most interested in 20th-century trains, especially diesels, so we struggled to find some of the early steam—I would have liked to include one more mid-1800s British steamer.

How realistic is the game?

I think at the high level it's pretty realistic. The scenarios tend to play fairly close to the way things developed in the real world, and the feel of the era is definitely there.

Of course, we had to make all kinds of concessions to playability, most notably in the area of scale. A real railroad has hundreds of trains, each with dozens of cars, each making many many trips per year. Obviously, we scaled everything back, often on a 100 to 1 ratio or more, but I think by efficiently operating 12 trains with 6 cars each, you get a pretty good feel for the problems confronting the real railroads which operate 1,200 trains with 60 cars each.

Did you have to fib in places in order not to sacrifice gameplay over historical accuracy?

The "Whistle Stops and Promises" campaign is a fib—Teddy Roosevelt did not make that trip, but he made those kinds of trips, as did other politicians. We fibbed on some of the details, but I think we're broadly accurate on the big picture—certainly more so than any other train game I've seen, or most any other computer game simulating broad events occurring over such a long time span.

Now that it's finished, how do you feel about it, and what do you like best?

First, I feel relieved that it's done.

Second, I'm really happy with it, on pretty much all levels. It definitely exceeds the goals I had when we started the project, and I'm really excited about the reception we've gotten for both the demo, and the final version, which has now been out for about a week.

Probably the thing I enjoy the most is the 3D terrain. It was one of the first things completed in the game, and I chose some different paths with the engine than the rest of the industry has embraced. I'm really happy with the result.

Can you tell us a few things about the game's AI? What makes it tick? What should a gamer watch out for?

The thing that most people have noticed is that the AI is solid, though not flashy, with its track building and operations, but usually does even better in the stock market.

Basically, computers do worse than humans with pattern recognition, and better than humans with mathematical formulas and pure calculation.

Track layout and train routing is essentially a pattern recognition problem. There's a complex map, with all sorts of "treasures" on it. Determine the best route for now, that leaves open expansion for the future. The AI is competent at this, though a skilled player

will generally be more efficient.

Stock buying is basically a formula. Factor in all the underlying numbers about a stock (earnings, revenue, asset value, and so on), compute an expected value, then compare it against the actual stock price. If the actual value is significantly higher than the stock price, buy. If it's significantly lower, sell. It's essentially a formula, and the computer is quite clever at it.

So the moral is, protect yourself on the stock market side by steadily buying up your own stock, keeping the price high, and discouraging the computer from buying up your stock. Manage your operations smartly and efficiently, and you should outperform the AI there. With majority control of the most efficient company on the map, you should be in great shape.

What are your favorite trains and strategies and why?

I like the American early, the Shay in the Mountains, the Pacific around 1900, and the GG-1 if I can afford electrification in the 1930s. By the time you reach the 1950s and beyond, almost all the trains are good. It's always fun to run the Mag-Lev if you can afford it, though it's not terribly cost efficient.

I definitely like to use the industrial cargoes, preferably where I can run complete transportation chains (from the mine to the factory to the city with the final goods). The best strategy is to look for a city that has nearby resources that can easily be used. Lay your track primarily on the basis of available resources, but then add more value by hauling passengers and mail, as they are available and appropriate.

Now that the game is out, are there any plans for add-on packs? What can the fans look forward to?

We're looking at a number of unannounced things now, some of which may be officially announced by the time folks read this. I think it's quite likely there will be an expansion product of some kind. In *Railroad Tycoon II* we focused on 1830 to 1920. I don't think we spent as much time on the modern era as we could have. Also, I like the unusual scenarios like "Whistle Stops and Promises," and would like to see more scenarios that break the mold like that one.

We're also looking at a number of possibilities to bring *Railroad Tycoon II* to other platforms aside from the PC, and I think it's pretty likely we'll see some ports in the next year.

The gaming community increasingly seems to be split into hardcore gamers for whom gameplay is everything and "technology gamers," whose passion for games is directed at hardware rather than gameplay. Where do you see the future of gaming headed amidst the technological flashes that characterize much of today's games? Will technology or creativity gain the upper hand?

Creativity—absolutely.

The technology buffs make a lot of noise, but if you look at the really big hits of the past few years—million sellers like *Myst, Doom, Command & Conquer, Warcraft II, Diablo, Age of Empires, Deer Hunter*—you'll see that most of them have good technology, but not bleeding edge stuff. Only Doom really falls into that category, and even it succeeded in large part thanks to a fun and creative design as much as its technology.

The problem is that the industry "insiders" both in the game development community and in the gaming press get all lathered up about the latest tri-linear filtering technique and whether a game uses Gouraud shading or Phong shading, but 80 percent of the people who buy games don't give a hoot. They want a fun game that'll play on the $1,000 computer they bought last Christmas and that's easy to get into.

What are some of the factors that make a good computer/strategy game?

Fun, fun, fun (as the Beach Boys would say).

The problem is that fun is hard to create according to a formula. The basic ingredients of fun for a computer game are:

* Good graphics and sound
* An interesting, reasonably novel premise
* Easy-to-learn, hard-to-master game mechanics
* Interactivity—players are presented with interesting, non-obvious choices which have meaningful impacts on the game's outcome.

What is (are) your favorite game(s) and why?

Well, I've already mentioned *Civilization* and *Railroad Tycoon 1*. More recently, I'd vote for *Panzer General*, *Total Annihilation*, and *Fallout*.

Basically, all of these games meet the criteria I just listed (or at least they did when released).

The gaming industry has become a tough battleground between corporate publishers. The industry economics are increasingly shaped in the image of the music and film industry. Games have to be released by a certain date or the publisher threatens to lose ground to the competition. Are the days of the independent producer/designers gone for good? Can the vision of the designer still rule in a world based on warfare by being the "first-to-market"?

Well, let me see how *Railroad Tycoon II* sells before I answer that!

Seriously, I think if anything the trend towards smaller, independent development houses is increasing. Almost all of the major hits of the last two to three years were developed by small shops, usually with five to fifty employees. When a big publisher buys a small shop, often much of the talent flees within a year or two (witness Raven, Papyrus, Bullfrog, and so on). Record labels don't buy the Rolling Stones—they sign deals to distribute their records, advance the group some money to make the record, and generally behave as independent entities. That's the future of this business, too.

Who worked harder?

The Team Behind Railroad Tycoon II

LOOKING AT THE FINAL GAME, IT'S HARD TO

BELIEVE THAT RAILROAD TYCOON II OWES ITS

EXISTENCE TO ONLY SIX DEDICATED

INDIVIDUALS, WHO LOST SLEEP FOR MONTHS

ON END TO BRING YOU WHAT IS ONE OF THE

FINEST STRATEGY GAMES IN RECENT YEARS.

HERE THEY ARE—THE TRUE RAILROAD

TYCOONS, INCLUDING THEIR ROLE ON THE

PROJECT, THEIR FAVORITE MULTIPLAYER

STRATEGIES, AND THEIR FAVORITE GAMES.

TODD BERGANTZ

ROLE ON THE PROJECT:	Initial World Artist, model construction, 3D and landscape artist, technical and hardware assistance, builder of office furniture and cleaner of toilets, requisite doomsayer and pessimistic influence, Quake champion, target for ridicule
FAVORITE THING ABOUT THE GAME:	The Station detail. Hey, I can be proud of my work.
FAVORITE STRATEGY:	Start a company, watch to see where your competitors lay their track, select bulldozer, and then bulldoze the likely major industries before they can put their station down, effectively making their track a waste. Not a very good strategy, mind you, but a fun one.
MEMORABLE MOMENT DURING DEVELOPMENT:	Sleeping at the office during the last month. It sucked. Also listening to Paul scream and create new obscenities as I stomp on him in *Quake I* and *II* stress-breaker sessions. Now, *that's* amusing...
CRUNCH TIME FOOD:	Chinese food
THINGS TO AVOID DURING CRUNCH TIME:	Mentioning in-game typos to Phil
FAVORITE GAMES BESIDES RT2:	*X-Wing, NHL 98/99, Total Annihilation, Carmageddon, Quake II, Gunship 2000*

DAVID DEEN

ROLE ON THE PROJECT:	World Artist: train clean up (the Train Man), logos, b/w cursors, some ground effects and beach animation
FAVORITE THING ABOUT THE GAME:	The ability to merge in multiplayer—the closest thing to conquering your enemy in battle!
FAVORITE STRATEGY:	Don't play against Phil. Otherwise, expand and act fast to get the best start. Don't be afraid to crowd into someone else's city and steal their passengers.
MEMORABLE MOMENT DURING DEVELOPMENT:	We finally started to test multiplayer. I thought I was doing decently and suddenly—BAM—Franz merged and took me over!
CRUNCH TIME FOOD:	No snack, just lots and lots of diet Coke. Well, OK, Cheese Nips aren't bad either.
THINGS TO AVOID DURING CRUNCH TIME:	Not taking the time to occasionally do other stuff like go swimming, read a book, or otherwise get out the RT2 world to "reboot."
FAVORITE GAMES BESIDES RT2:	*Civilization*

FRANZ J. FELSL

ROLE ON THE PROJECT:	Research, scenario design, and maps
FAVORITE THING ABOUT THE GAME:	Setting up pretty train rides through the mountains that waste yourprecious time. I enjoy the "train set" type put n' play ability that lets you build a model railroad. I don't have room at home for a train set, so this is my best alternative.
FAVORITE STRATEGY:	I like to buy everyone's industries just as they place their stations. AFTER they place their station is the key, as it indicates an investment on your competitors part. Also, whenever possible I try and buy up all my own stock, often taking bonds out to buy up company stock with company money. This makes you a very hard target for a hostile merge.
MEMORABLE MOMENT DURING DEVELOPMENT:	I was working late and there was a storm moving in from the northeast. I was going through an event bug list trying to find a coat for the Queen of Austria. Well, one thing lead to another and then...hey wait! This isn't amusing or interesting. Is this thing on?
CRUNCH TIME FOOD:	Little Debbie™ Swiss Rolls. A lot of snout for little cash.
THINGS TO AVOID DURING CRUNCH TIME:	Sleep
FAVORITE GAMES BESIDES RT2:	*Fallout, Transportation Tycoon, Defender of the Crown, Masters of Magic*

FRANK LUTZ

ROLE ON THE PROJECT:	World art, animations, video, video research, map design, travel arrangements, and pizza boy
FAVORITE THING ABOUT THE GAME:	The Pause button.
FAVORITE STRATEGY:	The Pause button. Actually, I like taking out a series of bonds right out the gate to buy up as much of my own stock as possible. This gives me a little breathing room so I don't have to worry about Todd badgering me with futile attempts to take over my company. All this upfront cash also allows me the ability to purchase industries that I notice my opponents are laying track to. Parasitic, I know, but most business is.
MEMORABLE MOMENT DURING DEVELOPMENT:	Meeting Sid Meier and Chris Taylor at E3 in Atlanta—the two men who have assured me no life outside their games.
CRUNCH TIME FOOD:	Raspberry Poptarts, Brisk Nestea, watermelon Bubble Yum after eating the most perverse flavored gas station beef jerky.
THINGS TO AVOID DURING CRUNCH TIME:	Phil's coffee
FAVORITE GAMES BESIDES RT2:	*Total Annihilation, Battlezone,* and *Quake II*

PAUL MULLEN

ROLE ON THE PROJECT:	I suppose you can call me the interface artist (player detail, intro screens, engine detail screens, pop-up screens, and so on) and sound effect creator. However, the role I wanted to fill was Bigfoot specialist, and bad joke teller (What did Spock find in the toilet? ...The Captain's log.).
FAVORITE THING ABOUT THE GAME:	The breaking glass in the campaign screen; "Hey! Get away from those winders!" I love the depth.
FAVORITE STRATEGY:	Survival. Get those two stations built and two trains pulling passengers quickly. Buy back stock in your company detail, if you know the people you're playing against will try to buy up all your stocks. It will keep upping the price of stocks and you'll make money. I still lose, but I survive longer.
MEMORABLE MOMENT DURING DEVELOPMENT:	I got engaged.
CRUNCH TIME FOOD:	Anything I could get my hands on.
THINGS TO AVOID DURING CRUNCH TIME:	Phil. He needed to concentrate 100 percent on programming.
FAVORITE GAMES BESIDES RT2:	*Quake II, Total Annihilation, Links Golf 98, NHL 98,* and I still love *Doom*

PHIL STEINMEYER

ROLE ON THE PROJECT:	Programmer, designer, producer
FAVORITE THING ABOUT THE GAME:	Train crashes and going all out on margin, then save your butt as your stock falls.
FAVORITE STRATEGY:	Start with as little outside investment as possible. Then, build a small, very short line. Get a little money coming in, and start issuing bonds to expand. Refinance the bonds a few years later.
MEMORABLE MOMENT DURING DEVELOPMENT:	The most awesome thing was when we were able to acquire the Railroad Tycoon name, which I didn't expect. The second most awesome thing was when we announced the game and released screen shots and got such an enthusiastic response. I knew then we were on the right track.
CRUNCH TIME FOOD:	Kit-Kat Bar™
THINGS TO AVOID DURING CRUNCH TIME:	Eating, sleeping, anything but programming
FAVORITE GAMES BESIDES RT2:	*Civilization, Total Annihilation, Quake II, Railroad Tycoon*

210

Freight Revenue Charts

TABLES A-1 AND A-2 PROVIDE USEFUL
INFORMATION FOR CALCULATING THE VALUE
OF YOUR CARGO. IN MOST CASES, YOU'LL BE
TOO BUSY TO WALK THROUGH THIS
CALCULATION FOR EVERY LOAD, BUT WHEN
THE CARGO IS LUCRATIVE, A LITTLE EXTRA
STUDY GOES A LONG WAY.

TABLE A-1 IS A QUICK REFERENCE FOR
CALCULATING THE VALUE OF A PARTICULAR HAUL.
USE IT TO FIGURE OUT HOW TO OPTIMIZE YOUR
LOADS. THIS TABLE WILL BE PARTICULARLY USEFUL
WHEN A RECESSION HITS.

TABLE A-1. FREIGHT REVENUE CALCULATOR

CARGO	BASE VALUE	DELIVERY TIME		DEMAND		MODIFIERS**
		DAYS	ROT FACTOR*	BY TOWNS	BY CITIES	
ALUMINUM	$35,000	1300	3			
AUTOMOBILE	$49,000	800	6		Yes	
BAUXITE	$28,000	1600	2			
CATTLE	$37,000	800	5			
CEMENT	$38,000	800	3		Yes	
CHEMICAL	$37,000	800	5			Liquid storage
COAL	$28,000	1600	2		Until 1910	
COFFEE	$37,000	800	5	Until 1878	Until 1878	Grain silo
COTTON	$36,000	1100	4			Warehouse
DIESEL	$39,000	1100	4			
FERTILIZER	$35,000	1300	3			
FOOD	$58,000	600	6	Yes	Yes	
GOODS	$42,000	800	5	Yes	Yes	Warehouse
GRAIN	$28,000	1600	2			Grain silo
GRAVEL	$28,000	1600	2			
HAZARDOUS	$46,000	800	5			
IRON	$28,000	1600	2			
LOGS	$28,000	1600	2			
LUMBER	$35,000	1300	3	Yes	Yes	
MAIL	$70,000	300	10	Yes	Yes	Post office
MILK	$55,000	300	5	Until 1900	Until 1900	Refrigerated storage
OIL	$37,000	1100	3		Until 1910	Liquid storage
PAPER	$46,000	800	5		Yes	
PASSENGER	$60,000	500	8	Yes	Yes	
PRODUCE	$42,000	600	6	Until 1878	Until 1878	Refrigerated storage
PULPWOOD	$28,000	1600	2			
RUBBER	$28,000	1600	2			
STEEL	$35,000	1300	3			
SUGAR	$37,000	800	5			Grain silo
TIRES	$35,000	1300	3			
URANIUM	$43,000	800	6			
WOOL	$36,000	1100	4			Warehouse

* The higher the number, the higher the rate of value deterioration.

** Will influence the deterioration rate of the associated cargo.

The figures in Table A-1 assume basic values of demanded cargo. Table A-2 should be your additional reference point if the cargo is not demanded, or if the demand value is higher or lower. It shows the percentage of valued return per rate of demand in each level of game play.

TABLE A-2. DEMANDS

DEMAND LEVEL	BASIC	ADVANCED	EXPERT
None	80%	50%	20%
0	100%	100%	50%
1	100%	100%	60%
2	100%	100%	70%
3	100%	100%	80%
4	100%	100%	90%
5	100%	100%	100%
6	100%	100%	110%
7	100%	100%	120%
8	100%	100%	130%
9	100%	100%	140%

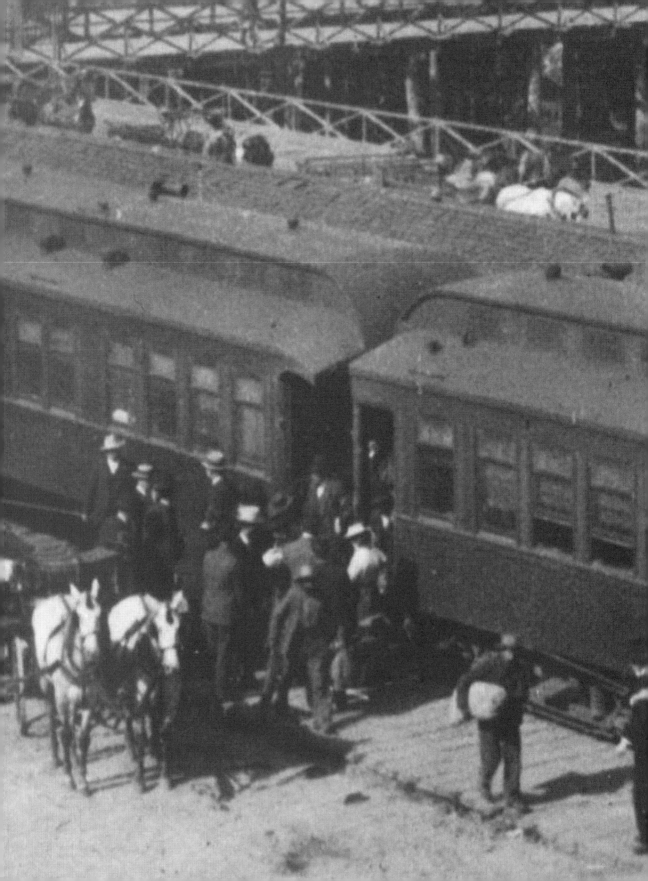

Train Charts

WITH 60 LOCOMOTIVES TO CHOOSE FROM,
YOU NEED TO QUANTIFY YOUR CHOICES. IT IS
BEST TO SELECT A TRAIN BASED ON ALL OF THE
REQUIREMENTS OF THE RUN YOU HAVE IN
MIND. WHILE A GENERALIST APPROACH MAY
APPLY AT TIMES, TO GET THE BEST RESULTS
YOU'LL NEED TO GET THE RIGHT LOCOMOTIVE
FOR THE JOB. TABLE B-1 WILL GIVE YOU ALL OF
THE INFORMATION YOU'LL NEED TO MAKE AN
INFORMED CHOICE. NOTE: WHILE THE
NUMBERS ARE REASONABLY ACCURATE FOR THE
LOCOMOTIVES LISTED, VARIANTS OCCUR AND
MODIFICATION TO PERFORMANCE WAS
ADJUSTED IN SOME CASES TO PROVIDE BETTER
GAME PLAY.

HERE'S HOW TO READ THE CHART:
A = NORTH AMERICAN AVAILABILITY; E = EUROPEAN
AVAILABILITY; W = WORLD AVAILABILITY; (NOTE: THESE WILL
NOT ALWAYS BE AVAILABLE IN EVERY SCENARIO) TYPE = TYPE OF
ENGINE; P = ELECTRIC POWER; D = DIESEL POWER; S = STEAM
POWER; FIRST = THE FIRST TIME THE LOCOMOTIVE WILL BE
AVAILABLE FOR SALE IN THE GAME; LAST = THE LAST TIME THE
LOCOMOTIVE WILL BE AVAILABLE FOR SALE IN THE GAME;
MAINT(ENANCE) AND FUEL = THE ANNUAL COST FOR THESE
ITEMS; (#@%) = THE # IS WEIGHT IN TONS OF THE CARGO LOAD,
THE % IS THE PERCENT OF GRADE BEING TRAVERSED. SPECIAL
NOTE: ALL NUMBERS ARE BASE LEVEL AND CAN BE MODIFIED BY
DATE, SCENARIO, MANAGERS AND MAPS.

TABLE B-1. THE TRAINS

NAME	A	E	W	T	FIRST	LAST	COST	MAINT.
Trevithick-1		E		S	1800	1835	$10,000	$6,000
Stephenson Rocket	A	E	W	S	1829	1851	$16,000	$6,000
2-4-0 John Bull	A	E	W	S	1831	1853	$23,000	$7,000
0-4-0 Dewitt Clinton	A	E	W	S	1833	1855	$18,000	$5,000
4-2-0 Prussian	A	E	W	S	1837	1857	$35,000	$8,000
4-4-0 American-C	A	E	W	S	1848	1885	$46,000	$5,000
4-2-2 Iron Duke	A	E	W	S	1855	1895	$78,000	$9,000
4-4-0 8-Wheeler	A	E	W	S	1868	1903	$59,000	$5,000
2-4-0 Vulcan	A	E	W	S	1872	1900	$32,000	$4,000
2-8-0 Consolidation	A	E	W	S	1877	1905	$51,000	$8,000
3-Truck Shay	A	E	W	S	1882	1930	$43,000	$17,000
4-8-0 Mastodon	A	E	W	S	1890	1911	$60,000	$13,000
4-6-0 Ten-Wheeler	A	E	W	S	1892	1911	$66,000	$11,000
2-6-0 Mogul	A	E	W	S	1895	1915	$83,000	$12,000
1-3 B_oB_o	A	E	W	P	1895	1935	$85,000	$6,000
4-4-2 Atlantic	A	E	W	S	1902	1929	$93,000	$18,000
2-6-0 Camelback	A	E	W	S	1905	1932	$75,000	$9,000
4-6-2 Pacific	A	E	W	S	1908	1945	$119,000	$21,000
0-10-0 Class G10		E	W	S	1910	1939	$98,000	$38,000
2-6-2 Prairie	A	E	W	S	1912	1953	$85,000	$11,000
4-4-0 D16sb	A	E	W	S	1914	1934	$65,000	$9,000
2-10-0 Class 13 H		E	W	S	1917	1940	$102,000	$36,000
USRA 0-6-0	A	E		S	1918	1942	$90,000	$13,000
2-8-2 Mikado	A	E	W	S	1919	1950	$133,000	$32,000
Be 4/6 II		E	W	P	1920	1950	$61,000	$11,000
4-6-0 Class B12	A	E	W	S	1923	1939	$146,000	$14,000
Ee 3/3	A	E	W	P	1923	1948	$47,000	$7,000
Class 1045	A	E	W	P	1927	1950	$95,000	$6,000
USRA 0-8-0	A	E	W	S	1930	1948	$98,000	$18,000
Class A4 Mallard		E	W	S	1935	1955	$200,000	$19,000

Fuel	Acceleration	Reliability	0@ 0%	150@ 0%	300@ 0%	150@ 4%	300@ 4%
$7,543	Extremely Poor	Extremely Poor	10	5	2	1	1
$7,992	Extremely Poor	Below Average	15	6	3	1	1
$9,256	Poor	Below Average	25	11	5	1	1
$7,187	Extremely Poor	Poor	20	13	8	1	1
$10,622	Extremely Poor	Below Average	30	16	8	1	1
$12,606	Poor	Above Average	42	26	15	1	1
$30,736	Poor	Below Average	54	37	23	3	1
$17,808	Below Average	Above Average	48	33	20	3	1
$6,393	Very Poor	Below Average	30	20	12	2	1
$19,512	Below Average	Good	40	31	22	6	1
$18,227	Poor	Good	15	14	13	10	7
$22,995	Very Poor	Poor	45	36	27	9	2
$21,727	Below Average	Below Average	50	38	26	6	1
$25,131	Average	Average	50	38	27	7	1
$33,116	Poor	Poor	55	44	33	13	3
$43,556	Fast	Above Average	80	49	28	3	1
$15,000	Poor	Very Good	30	27	24	15	9
$62,516	Above Average	Average	95	66	44	8	1
$50,521	Above Average	Average	50	47	34	9	2
$34,157	Below Average	Good	60	49	35	9	2
$21,024	Poor	Very Good	45	36	27	9	2
$46,289	Above Average	Good	40	36	32	21	12
$29,993	Poor	Good	40	37	30	12	4
$51,072	Above Average	Good	55	50	45	31	19
$14,701	Fast	Very Good	35	31	26	14	6
$32,407	Fast	Above Average	71	51	33	6	1
$11,880	Very Poor	Good	31	29	26	20	14
$11,636	Fast	Above Average	40	36	33	23	14
$32,236	Below Average	Above Average	45	40	35	20	10
$55,136	Above Average	Below Average	126	92	53	6	1

NAME	A	E	W	T	FIRST	LAST	COST	MAINT
GG1	A		W	P	1935	1970	$285,000	$19,000
Class E18		E	W	P	1936	1966	$97,000	$16,000
4-6-4 Hudson	A	E	W	S	1937	1953	$210,000	$25,000
4-8-4 Daylight	A	E	W	S	1937	1952	$230,000	$30,000
4-6-4 J3A Streamliner	A	E	W	S	1938	1955	$255,000	$28,000
Ae 8/14		E	W	P	1939	1955	$210,000	$24,000
4-8-8-4 Big Boy	A			S	1941	1955	$375,000	$75,000
Class 1020		E	W	P	1941	1981	$119,000	$18,000
4-4-4-4 T-1	A		W	S	1945	9999	$284,000	$28,000
F3A+B	A	E	W	D	1945	1968	$265,000	$16,000
Alco PA-1	A	E	W	D	1946	1990	$210,000	$16,000
F9	A	E	W	D	1949	1970	$337,000	$18,000
GP9	A	E	W	D	1954	1980	$165,000	$11,000
E 69		E	W	D	1955	1970	$86,000	$8,000
GP18	A	E	W	D	1958	1975	$245,000	$15,000
V200		E	W	D	1959	1985	$160,000	$19,000
Penn. E44	A	E	W	P	1960	1985	$370,000	$22,000
Class 55 Deltic		E	W	D	1961	1981	$480,000	$15,000
Shinkansen Bullet		E	W	P	1966	2002	$650,000	$66,000
FP45	A	E	W	D	1968	9999	$366,000	$14,000
SD45	A	E	W	D	1972	1994	$360,000	$21,000
SDP40	A	E	W	D	1973	1989	$292,000	$18,000
E60CP	A			P	1973	1998	$260,000	$19,000
Class E111	A	E	W	P	1974	9999	$390,000	$17,000
E656 FS		E	W	P	1975	1995	$226,000	$17,000
Dash-9	A	E	W	D	1993	9999	$478,000	$18,000
AMD-103	A			D	1993	9999	$425,000	$25,000
Thalys Bullet	A	E	W	P	1994	9999	$1,000,000	$78,000
Class 232	A	E	W	D	1997	9999	$492,000	$35,000
MaglevTBX-1	A	E	W	P	2008	9999	$2,500,000	$200,000

FUEL	ACCELERATION	RELIABILITY	0@ 0%	150@ 0%	300@ 0%	150@ 4%	300@ 4%
$42,721	Above Average	Outstanding	100	87	74	43	20
$27,493	Fast	Good	93	66	44	11	1
$54,017	Below Average	Average	90	76	62	27	10
$63,611	Average	Below Average	80	70	61	33	17
$112,234	Above Average	Poor	103	89	67	23	6
$47,906	Fast	Above Average	68	64	60	46	34
$88,040	Above Average	Poor	68	67	62	48	35
$21,545	Fast	Very Good	56	51	45	31	18
$78,213	Fast	Good	85	73	59	26	10
$52,015	Fast	Above Average	85	79	65	30	12
$52,800	Average	Average	90	77	64	35	15
$63,749	Above Average	Above Average	110	94	78	43	19
$48,028	Average	Good	71	64	56	36	20
$12,837	Fast	Below Average	31	29	28	24	19
$55,131	Above Average	Very Good	83	76	69	50	32
$53,878	Above Average	Below Average	87	77	66	40	20
$37,971	Fast	Average	70	63	56	38	22
$52,155	Below Average	Very Good	100	87	73	41	19
$66,680	Virtually Instant	Average	130	93	61	16	2
$65,740	Above Average	Above Average	106	82	54	14	2
$36,009	Average	Average	65	59	53	37	22
$61,966	Above Average	Poor	103	89	75	43	19
$38,043	Very Fast	Average	85	74	64	38	18
$38,016	Average	Good	85	79	72	54	37
$37,734	Average	Above Average	93	77	60	24	8
$68,410	Above Average	Good	70	65	60	46	31
$88,068	Very Fast	Above Average	105	86	68	32	11
$111,756	Virtually Instant	Below Average	186	133	88	23	3
$72,625	Very Fast	Very Good	75	69	62	46	29
$274,139	Instant	Above Average	280	192	120	26	3

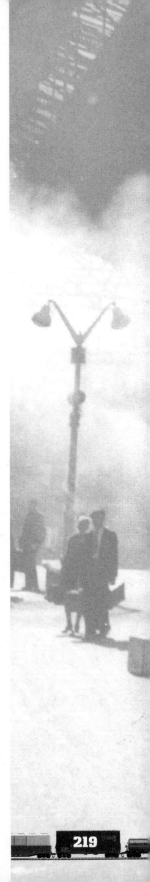

Functions and Effects

THE TABLES BELOW COVER VARIOUS ASPECTS OF USING BOTH FUNCTIONS AND EFFECTS IN YOUR LEVELS. THE FUNCTION NAME APPEARS IN THE LEFT-HAND COLUMN. PARAMETERS LISTS ANY ADDITIONAL PARAMETERS, AND NOTES PROVIDES A BRIEF DESCRIPTION OF THAT FUNCTION.

TABLE C-1. FUNCTIONS

FUNCTION NAME	PARAMETERS	NOTES
CompanyBookValue	Optional - Class	Company total assets minus debt, i.e. the shareholder's equity
CompanyCash	Optional - Class	The cash on hand of a company
CompanyDebt	Optional - Class	The total debt of a company (All bonds, plus negative cash, if cash is negative); for a company with one $500,000 bond and cash of -$34,000, this would evaluate to 534000
CompanyDoubleTrackCells	Optional - Class	The number of cells of double track owned by this company
CompanyElectricTrackCells	Optional - Class	The number of cells of electric track owned by this company
CompanyGoodwill	Optional - Class	The goodwill of this company
CompanyId	Optional - Class	The ID of this company. Each company has a unique ID that never changes. In the editor, you can see company IDs on the list box at the bottom of the main screen; they are the number just to the left of the company name, i.e. for 2) Union Pacific the id of that company is 2.
CompanyLoadsHauledLifetime	Optional - Class	Number of car loads hauled in lifetime by this company
CompanyLoadsHauledThisYear	Optional - Class	Number of car loads hauled this year by this company
CompanyNetIncomeLifetime	Optional - Class	Company's net income for its entire lifetime
CompanyNetIncomeThisYear	Optional - Class	Company's net income for this year only
CompanyRevenueLifetime	Optional - Class	Company's revenue for its entire lifetime
CompanyRevenueThisYear	Optional - Class	Company's revenue for this year only
CompanySingleTrackCells	Optional - Class	The number of cells of single track owned by this company
CompanyTerritoryConnectedToCity	Required (ID)	Pass in the ID of the city you want to test against; True if there is a station controlled by the current company within the current territory and the target city that can trace a continuous route of track to the other territory; track ownership does not matter
CompanyTerritoryConnectedToTerritory	Required (ID)	Pass in the ID of the territory you want to test against; True if there is a station controlled by the current company within each territory that can trace a continuous route of track to the other territory; track ownership does not matter.
CompanyTerritoryGoodwill	Optional - Class	The goodwill of a company in the current territory

FUNCTION NAME	PARAMETERS	NOTES
CompanyTerritoryHasAnyAccess	Optional - Class	True if the company can do any of the above 4 items
CompanyTerritoryHasBuildingBuyAccess	Optional - Class	True if the company can buy buildings in the current territory
CompanyTerritoryHasStationAccess	Optional - Class	True if the company can build stations in the current territory
CompanyTerritoryHasTrackAccess	Optional - Class	True if the company can lay track through the current territory
CompanyTerritoryHasTrainAccess	Optional - Class	True if the company can run trains through the current territory
CompanyTerritoryLoadsHauledBetweenTerritory	Optional - Class	The number of car loads hauled between to specified territories
CompanyTerritoryLoadsHauledLifetime	Optional - Class	The number of car loads hauled lifetime TO (not from) the current territory
CompanyTerritoryLoadsHauledLifetimeFromTerritory	Optional - Class	The number of car loads hauled lifetime to specified territory from a specified territory
CompanyTerritoryLoadsHauledThisYear	Optional - Class	The number of car loads hauled this year TO (not from) the current territory
CompanyTerritoryTrackCells	Optional - Class	The number of cells of track the company has in the current territory
CompanyTotalAssets	Optional - Class	Total assets of a company, including cash (if positive), track, trains, and so on; debt is not subtracted from this number; to get net assets, subtract CompanyDebt from CompanyTotalAssets
CompanyTrackCells	Optional - Class	The number of cells of track owned by this company
CompanyVariable1	Optional - Class	A wildcard variable you can set up as a result of one event that can affect the triggers of other events; a unique set of these variables is saved for each company
CompanyVariable2	Optional - Class	A wildcard variable
CompanyVariable3	Optional - Class	A wildcard variable
CompanyVariable4	Optional - Class	A wildcard variable
False	None	Evaluates to false (false is represented internally as the number 0)
GameDoubleTrackCells	None	The number of cells of double track
GameEconomicState	None	The current game economy, ranges from 0 to 4, with 0 being depression and 4 being boom times
GameElectricTrackCells	None	The number of cells of electric track
GameExistsCompanyId	Required (ID)	True if the company with the ID specified in the parameter is actively in the game
GameExistsPlayerId	Required (ID)	True if the player with the ID specified in the parameter is actively in the game
GameIsMultiplayer	Required	True if he game is set for multiplayer
GameIsNotMultiplayer	Required	True if he game is *not* set for multiplayer

Function Name	Parameters	Notes
GameLoadsHauledLifetime	None	The number of car loads hauled by all companies since the beginning of the game
GameLoadsHauledThisYear	None	The number of car loads hauled by all companies this year. Empty cars don't count. The distance hauled does not matter for the purposes of this and similar functions
GameMonth	None	The current month the game is in
GameNumCompanies	None	The number of active companies in the game; liquidated companies don't count
GameNumPlayers	None	The number of computer and human players actively in the game (basically, the number of players the human chose to have in the game on the setup screen)
GameSingleTrackCells	None	The number of cells of single track
GameStartYear	None	The year this game started
GameTrackCells from all companies	None	The number of cells of track in existence
GameVariable1	None	A wildcard variable you can set up as a result of one event that can affect the triggers of other events
GameVariable2	None	A wildcard variable
GameVariable3	None	A wildcard variable
GameVariable4	None	A wildcard variable
GameYear	None	The current year the game is in
GameYearMonth	None	The current year and month the game is in, handily combined into a single variable—if the current date was July, 1865, this would evaluate to 186507
GameYearsElapsedSinceStart	None	The number of years elapsed in the game; for the first 12 months, this evaluates to 0; for the next 12 months, to 1; and so on
PlayerCash	Optional - Class	Cash for the current player
PlayerControlledCompanyId	Optional - Class	Returns the ID of the company the player currently controls (0 if the player controls no company)
PlayerControlsAnyCompany	Optional - Class	True if the player is currently chairman of any company
PlayerId	Optional - Class	The ID of this player; each player has a unique ID that never changes; in the editor, you can see player IDs on the list box at the bottom of the main screen; they are the number just to the left of the player name; for example, for 3) Jay Gould—that player's ID is 3
PlayerNetWorth	Optional - Class	Total net worth for the current player the sum of the above 2 items.
PlayerStockValue	Optional - Class	Value of stock holdings for the current player

FUNCTION NAME	PARAMETERS	NOTES
PlayerVariable1	Optional - Class	A wildcard variable you can set up as a result of one event that can affect the triggers of other events; a unique set of these variables is saved for each player
PlayerVariable2	Optional - Class	A wildcard variable
PlayerVariable3	Optional - Class	A wildcard variable
PlayerVariable4	Optional - Class	A wildcard variable
Random1To10000	None	Generates a random number between 1 and 10000
TerritoryConnectedToCity	Required (ID)	Pass in the ID of the city you want to test against; true if there is a station within the current territory and the target city that can trace a continuous route of track to the other territory, regardless of which company owns the track or stations
TerritoryConnectedToTerritory	Required (ID)	Pass in the ID of the territory you want to test against; true if there is a station within each territory that can trace a continuous route of track to the other territory, regardless of which company owns the track or stations
TerritoryId	Optional - Class	The ID of this player; each territory has a unique ID that never changes. In the editor, you can see territory IDs on the listbox at the bottom of the main screen, as you paint territories. They are the number just to the left of the player name; for example, for 3) Germany—that territory's ID is 3
TerritoryLoadsHauledLifetime	Optional - Class	The number of car loads hauled by all companies TO this territory since the start of the game (loads hauled FROM the territory don't count)
TerritoryLoadsHauledThisYear	Optional - Class	The number of car loads hauled by all companies TO this territory this year (loads hauled FROM the territory don't count)
TerritoryTrackCells	Optional - Class	The number of cells of track from all companies in the current territory
TerritoryVariable1	Optional - Class	A wildcard variable you can set up as a result of one event that can affect the triggers of other events; a unique set of these variables is saved for each territory
TerritoryVariable2	Optional - Class	A wildcard variable
TerritoryVariable3	Optional - Class	A wildcard variable
TerritoryVariable4	Optional - Class	A wildcard variable
True	None	Evaluates to true of course

TABLE C-2. EFFECTS FUNCTIONS

EFFECT	RANGE	NOTES
Game Over - Win 1 (instant)	on/off	This is the last place finish
Game Over - Win 2 (instant)	on/off	This is the second place finish
Game Over - Win 3 (instant)	on/off	This is the first place finish
Game Over - Loss (instant)	on/off	This is the loss trigger
Company Cash (instant)	Variable $	
Player Cash (instant)	Variable $	
Economic Status (instant)	-4 to +4 levels	4 being the best, -4 the worst
Acceleration	Variable % -99 to +100	
Acceleration - Diesel	Variable % -99 to +100	
Acceleration - Electric	Variable % -99 to +100	
Acceleration -Steam	Variable % -99 to +100	
Bridge Building	Variable % -99 to +100	
Building Buy Cost	Variable % -99 to +100	
Company Overhead	Variable % -99 to +100	
Credit Rating	-10 to +10 levels	10 being the best, -10 the worst
Diesel Engine Purchase	Variable % -99 to +100	
Electric Engine Purchase	Variable % -99 to +100	
Electric Track Building	Variable % -99 to +100	
Engine Maintenance	Variable % -99 to +100	
Engine Maintenance- Diesel	Variable % -99 to +100	
Engine Maintenance- Electric	Variable % -99 to +100	
Engine Maintenance- Steam	Variable % -99 to +100	
Engine Purchase	Variable % -99 to +100	
Fuel Costs	Variable % -99 to +100	
Fuel Costs - Diesel	Variable % -99 to +100	
Fuel Costs - Electric	Variable % -99 to +100	
Fuel Costs - Steam	Variable % -99 to +100	
Manager Salaries	Variable % -99 to +100	
Merger Premium	Variable % -99 to +100	
Mountainous Track Building	Variable % -99 to +100	
Political Savvy	Variable % -99 to +100	
Prime Rate	-5 to +5 levels	5 being the best, -5 the worst
Station Building	Variable % -99 to +100	

EFFECT	RANGE	NOTES
Station Turnaround	Variable % -99 to +100	
Steam Engine Purchase	Variable % -99 to +100	
Stock Prices	Variable % -99 to +100	
Track Building	Variable % -99 to +100	
Track Maintenance	Variable % -99 to +100	
Traction	Variable % -99 to +100	
Traction - Diesel	Variable % -99 to +100	
Traction - Electric	Variable % -99 to +100	
Traction - Steam	Variable % -99 to +100	
Train Safety	Variable % -99 to +100	
Train Speed	Variable % -99 to +100	
Train Speed - Diesel	Variable % -99 to +100	
Train Speed - Electric	Variable % -99 to +100	
Train Speed - Steam	Variable % -99 to +100	
Territory Allow all	All or Nothing	
Territory Allow Track Build	All or Nothing	
Territory Allow Train Run	All or Nothing	
Territory Allow Station Build	All or Nothing	
Territory Allow Building Buy	All or Nothing	
Territory Confiscate All (instant)	None or All	
Territory Confiscate Track (instant)	None or All	
Territory Confiscate Trains (instant)	None or All	
Territory Confiscate Stations(instant)	None or All	
Territory Confiscate Buildings (instant)	None or All	

TABLE C-3. EFFECTS CARGO AND ITEMS

EFFECT	RANGE	NOTES
All Passenger & Cargo Production	Variable % -99 to +100	All change the number produced each year.
All Passenger & Cargo Revenue	Variable % -99 to +100	see above
Aluminum Revenue	Variable % -99 to +100	see above
Aluminum Revenue	Variable % -99 to +100	see above
Auto Production	Variable % -99 to +100	see above
Auto Revenue	Variable % -99 to +100	see above
Bauxite Production	Variable % -99 to +100	see above
Bauxite Revenue	Variable % -99 to +100	see above
Cattle Production	Variable % -99 to +100	see above
Cattle Revenue	Variable % -99 to +100	see above
Cement Production	Variable % -99 to +100	see above
Cement Revenue	Variable % -99 to +100	see above
Chemical Production	Variable % -99 to +100	see above
Chemical Revenue	Variable % -99 to +100	see above
Coal Revenue	Variable % -99 to +100	see above
Coal Revenue	Variable % -99 to +100	see above
Coffee Revenue	Variable % -99 to +100	see above
Coffee Revenue	Variable % -99 to +100	see above
Cotton Production	Variable % -99 to +100	see above
Cotton Revenue	Variable % -99 to +100	see above
Diesel Production	Variable % -99 to +100	see above
Diesel Revenue	Variable % -99 to +100	see above
Fertilizer Production	Variable % -99 to +100	see above
Fertilizer Revenue	Variable % -99 to +100	see above
Food Production	Variable % -99 to +100	see above
Food Revenue	Variable % -99 to +100	see above
Goods Production	Variable % -99 to +100	see above
Goods Revenue	Variable % -99 to +100	see above
Grain Revenue	Variable % -99 to +100	see above
Grain Revenue	Variable % -99 to +100	see above
Gravel Production	Variable % -99 to +100	see above
Gravel Revenue	Variable % -99 to +100	see above
Iron Production	Variable % -99 to +100	see above
Iron Revenue	Variable % -99 to +100	see above
Log Production	Variable % -99 to +100	see above
Log Revenue	Variable % -99 to +100	see above

APPENDIXES